The Mother Tongue

Student Workbook 1
Answer Key

By
Amy M. Edwards and
Christina J. Mugglin

BLUE SKY DAISIES

Exercises taken from *The Mother Tongue Book II*
by George Lyman Kittredge, Sarah Louise Arnold © 1901, 1908

and *The Mother Tongue: Adapted for Modern Students* by Amy M. Edwards and Christina J. Mugglin © 2014

This answer key accompanies *The Mother Tongue Student Workbook 1*
by Amy M. Edwards and Christina J. Mugglin © 2014.

The Mother Tongue Student Workbook 1 Answer Key
By Amy M. Edwards and Christina J. Mugglin © 2014
Second printing, 2015

Published by Blue Sky Daisies
Wichita, Kansas
blueskydaisies.wordpress.com

Cover art: A detail from *Clouds* (1882), by John Constable

ISBN-13: 978-0-9905529-3-2
ISBN-10: 0990552934

The Mother Tongue
Adapted for Modern Students
Student Workbook 1 Answer Key

This book contains answers to the exercises from *The Mother Tongue: Adapted for Modern Students* which are also contained in the *The Mother Tongue Student Workbook 1*.

Nearly all of the exercises in *The Mother Tongue* are taken from great English writers of centuries past. Where possible, we have supplied the source for many of the sentences and passages used for practice exercises in *The Mother Tongue Book II*. In some instances, Kittredge and Arnold adapted quotations slightly, so they are not always exactly quoted from the original.

We have endeavored to record accurate answers to all of the grammar exercises in *The Mother Tongue Student Workbook 1*, however our efforts are constrained by our humanness. As Pope wrote, "To err is human; to forgive, divine." We beg your forgiveness for any errors you discover. You may contact us and let us know at blueskydaisies.wordpress.com.

Amy M. Edwards
Christina J. Mugglin
2014

Table of Contents

Chapter 1: General Principles

There are no written exercises given for chapter 1.

Chapter 2: The Parts of Speech

There are no written exercises given for chapter 2.

Chapter 3: Nouns

Students were instructed to underline the nouns and label the word C for common or P for proper.

1. Drake **P**
    ship **C**
    men **C**
    Straits of Magellan **P**
    Englishman **P**
    coast **C**
    Chili **P**
    Peru **P**
    bark **C**
    gold-dust **C**
    silver-ingots **C**
    Potosi **P**
    pearls **C**
    emeralds **C**
    diamonds **C**
    cargo **C**
    galleon **C**
    year **C**
    Lima **P**
    Cadiz **P**

    (John Richard Green (1837-1883),
    History of the English People*)*

2. village **C**
    houses **C**
    truth **C**
    years **C**
    country **C**
    province **C**
    Great Britain **P**
    fellow **C**
    name **C**
    Rip Van Winkle **P**
    descendant **C**
    Van Winkles **P**
    days **C**
    Peter Stuyvesant **P**
    siege **C**
    Fort Christina **P**

    (Washington Irving (1783-1859),
    "Rip Van Winkle")

3. inhabitant **C**
    Truro **P**
    fortnight **C**
    St. John **P**
    Cohasset **P**
    bodies **C**
    shore **C**
    Clay Pounds **P**

    (Henry David Thoreau (1817-1862),
    "The Highland Light")

4. Oliver Goldsmith **P**
    tenth **C**
    November **P**
    hamlet **C**
    Pallas **P**
    Pallasmore **P**
    county **C**
    Longford **P**
    Ireland **P**

    (Washington Irving (1783-1859),
    Oliver Goldsmith*)*

Chapter 4: Special Classes of Nouns

I.
The abstract and collective nouns are given and labeled.
1. number **C** people **C** *(Maria Edgeworth (1768-1849),* The Patronage*)*
2. band **C** *(William Shakespeare (1564-1616),* Titus Andronicus*)*
3. party **C** *(Jane Austen (1775-1817),* Sense and Sensibility*)*
4. reason **A** *(William Shakespeare (1564-1616),* King Richard II*)*
5. People **C** force **A** imagination **A** *(Daniel Defoe (1660-1731),* A Journal of the Plague Year*)*

6. <u>Senate</u> **C** *(William Shakespeare (1564-1616), Coriolanus)*
7. <u>reverence</u> **A** <u>place</u> **A** *(William Shakespeare (1564-1616), King Henry IV)*
8. <u>place</u> **A** <u>company</u> **C** <u>knowledge</u> **A** *(Philip Dormer Stanhope, Earl of Chesterfield (1694-1773), "Lord Chesterfield's Letters")*
9. <u>troop</u> **C** *(William Shakespeare (1564-1616), Othello)*
10. <u>courage</u> **A** *(William Shakespeare (1564-1616), Henry V)*
11. <u>family</u> **C** <u>repast</u> **A** *(Oliver Goldsmith (1730-1774), The Vicar of Wakefield)*
12. <u>society</u> **C** <u>place</u> **A** *(William Cowper (1731-1800), "Letters")*
13. <u>scorn</u> **A** *(William Shakespeare (1564-1616), Othello)*
14. <u>Senate</u> **C** *(William Shakespeare (1564-1616), Julius Caesar)*
15. <u>enemy</u> **A** <u>people</u> **C** <u>country</u> **C** *(William Shakespeare (1564-1616), Coriolanus)*
16. <u>Society</u> **C** <u>happiness</u> **A**
17. <u>army</u> **C** <u>multitude</u> **C** *(William Shakespeare (1564-1616), King Henry IV)*
18. <u>knowledge</u> **A** <u>wisdom</u> **A**
19. <u>country</u> **C** <u>hate</u> **A** *(William Shakespeare (1564-1616), King Henry IV)*
20. <u>Parliament</u> **C** *(William Shakespeare (1564-1616), King Henry IV)*
21. <u>number</u> **C** *(William Shakespeare (1564-1616), Antony and Cleopatra)*

II.
Answers will vary. Suggestions are given.

men	*company*		musicians	*ensemble, band, orchestra*
birds	*flock*		robbers	*band, gang*
cows	*herd*		pirates	*band, gang, crew*
thieves	*band, gang*		books	*library, stack*
marbles	*bag, collection*		postage stamps	*book, collection*
school children	*class*		senators	*Senate*
sailors	*crew*		Members of Congress	*Congress*
soldiers	*battalion*		partners in business	*partnership*
football players	*team*			

III.

true	*truth*		insane	*insanity*
false	*falsehood*		passionate	*passion*
good	*goodness*		natural	*nature*
bad	*badness*		hasty	*haste*
lazy	*laziness*		valiant	*valor*
careless	*carelessness*		angry	*anger*
free	*freedom*		grieving	*grief*
brave	*bravery*		sorry	*sorrow*
sinful	*sinfulness*		holy	*holiness*
cautious	*caution*		evil	*evilness*
just	*justice*		unjust	*injustice*
beautiful	*beauty*		accurate	*accuracy*
amiable	*amity*		simple	*simplicity*

Chapter 5: Pronouns

I.

Nouns and pronouns are underlined and labeled in the parentheses following. The pronoun's antecedent is given. The student should draw an arrow to that word.

1. **Goneril, (N)** the elder, declared that **she (P, Goneril)** loved **her (P, Goneril) father (N)** more than **words (N)** could give out, that **he (P, father)** was dearer to **her (P, Goneril)** than the **light (N)** of **her (P, Goneril)** own **eyes (N)**. *(Adapted from Charles and Mary Lamb's Tales from Shakespeare, "King Lear")*

2. **Bassanio (N)** took the **ring (N)** and vowed never to part with **it. (P, ring)**
(Adapted from Charles and Mary Lamb's Tales from Shakespeare, "Merchant of Venice")

3. The **floor (N)** of the **cave (N)** was dry and level, and had a sort of small loose **gravel (N)** upon **it. (P, floor)**
(Daniel Defoe (1660-1731), Robinson Crusoe)

4. Having now brought all my **things (N)** on **shore,(N)** and secured **them,(P, things) I (P)** went back to my **boat, (N)** and rowed, or paddled **her (P, boat)** along the **shore, (N)** to **her (P, boat)** old **harbor, (N)** where **I (P)** laid **her (P, boat)** up. *(Daniel Defoe (1660-1731), Robinson Crusoe)*

5. **Heaven (N)** lies about **us (P)** in **our (P, us) infancy. (N)** *(William Wordsworth (1770-1850), "Ode")*

6. Blessed is **he (P)** who has found **his (P) work. (N)** *(Thomas Carlyle (1795-1881), "The Modern Worker")*

7. In fact, **Tom (N)** declared **it (P)** was of no use to work on **his (P, Tom) farm (N)**; **it (P, farm)** was the most pestilent little **piece (N)**of **ground (N)** in the whole **country (N)**; **everything (N)** about **it (P, farm)** went wrong, and would go wrong, in spite of **him. (P, Tom)** *(Washington Irving (1783-1859), "Rip Van Winkle")*

8. When **Portia (N)** parted with **her (P, Portia) husband (N)**, **she (P, Portia)** spoke cheeringly to **him (P, husband)**, and bade **him (P, husband)** bring **his (P, husband)** dear **friend (N)** along with **him (P, husband)** when **he (P, husband)** returned. *(Adapted from Charles and Mary Lamb's Tales from Shakespeare, "Merchant of Venice")*

II.

Answers will vary, but students should provide an appropriate pronoun in the blank.

1. A thought struck __**him**__ , and __**he**__ wrote a letter to one of __**his**__ friends.

2. The flowers were bending __**their**__ heads, as if __**they**__ were dreaming of the rainbow and dew.
(George Prentice (1802-1870), "The Tempest")

3. We make way for the man who boldly pushes past __**us**__. *(Christian Bovee (1820-1904))*

4. "That's a brave man," said Wellington, when __**he**__ saw a soldier turn pale as __**he**__ marched against a battery: "__**He**__ knows __**his**__ danger, and faces __**it**__." *(Orison Swett Marden (1850-1924), Pushing to the Front)*

5. I know not what course others may take; but, as for __**me**__ , give __**me**__ liberty, or give __**me**__ death. *(Patrick Henry (1736-1799))*

6. There, in __**his**__ noisy mansion, skilled to rule,
The village master taught __**his**__ little school.
(Oliver Goldsmith (1730-1774), "The Village Schoolmaster")

7. Wordsworth helps us to live __**our**__ best and highest life; __**he**__ is a strengthening and purifying influence like __**his**__ own mountains. *(Lucy Helen Muriel Soulsby (1856-1927), Stray Thoughts on Reading)*

8. As the queen hesitated to pass on, young Raleigh, throwing __his__ cloak from his shoulder, laid __it__ on the miry spot, so as to ensure __her__ stepping over __it__ dryshod. (*Sir Walter Scott (1771-1832), History of Scotland*)

9. Tender-handed stroke a nettle,
   And __it__ stings you for __its__ pains;
   Grasp __it__ like a man of mettle,
   And __it__ soft as silk remains.
   (*Aaron Hill (1685-1750), "Verses Written on a Window in Scotland"*)

10. Whatever people may think of __you__, do that which __you__ believe to be right.

11. No man is so foolish but __he__ may give another good counsel sometimes, and no man so wise but __he__ may easily err. (*Ben Jonson (1572-1637), Explorata*)

Chapter 6: Verbs and Verb Phrases

I.

Verbs and verb phrases are underlined twice.

1. Count Otto <u>stares</u> till his eyelids <u>ache</u>. (*Winthrop Mackworth Praed (1802-1839), "The Bridal of Belmont"*)

2. But so slowly <u>did</u> I <u>creep</u> along, that I <u>heard</u> a clock in a cottage <u>strike</u> four before I <u>turned</u> down the lane from Slough to Eton. (*Thomas De Quincey (1785-1859), Beauties*)

3. Like as the waves <u>make</u> towards the pebbled shore,
   So <u>do</u> our minutes <u>hasten</u> to their end.
   (*William Shakespeare (1564-1616), "Sonnet 60"*)

4. If it <u>rains</u>, we <u>converse</u> within doors.

5. The book you <u>mention</u> <u>lies</u> now upon my table.

6. The fleet in the Downs <u>sent</u> their captains on shore, <u>hoisted</u> the King's pennon, and <u>blockaded</u> the Thames. (*John Richard Green (1837-1883), History of the English People*)

7. The little company of the "Pilgrim Fathers," as after-times <u>loved</u> to call them, <u>landed</u> on the barren coast of Massachusetts, at a spot to which they <u>gave</u> the name of Plymouth, in memory of the last English port at which they <u>touched</u>. (*John Richard Green (1837-1883), History of the English People*)

II.

Students were instructed to find verbs and verb phrases in chapter 5, Exercise II. The verbs and verbs phrases are shown below underlined twice. (Some infinitives and participles are shown in italics. These verb forms are not introduced until chapters 100 and 101.)

1. A thought <u>struck</u> __him__, and __he__ <u>wrote</u> a letter to one of __his__ friends.

2. The flowers <u>were bending</u> __their__ heads, as if __they__ <u>were dreaming</u> of the rainbow and dew. (*George Prentice (1802-1870), "The Tempest"*)

3. We <u>make</u> way for the man who boldly <u>pushes</u> past __us__. (*Christian Bovee (1820-1904)*)

4. "That<u>'s</u> a brave man," <u>said</u> Wellington, when __he__ <u>saw</u> a soldier <u>turn</u> pale as __he__ <u>marched</u> against a battery: "__He__ <u>knows</u> __his__ danger, and <u>faces</u> __it__." (*Orison Swett Marden (1850-1924), Pushing to the Front*)

5. I <u>know</u> not what course others <u>may take</u>; but, as for __**me**__ , <u>give</u> __**me**__ liberty, or <u>give</u> __**me**__ death. *(Patrick Henry (1736-1799))*

6. There, in __**his**__ noisy mansion, <u>skilled</u> *to rule*,
The village master <u>taught</u> __**his**__ little school.
(Oliver Goldsmith (1730-1774), "The Village Schoolmaster")

7. Wordsworth <u>helps</u> us *to live* __**our**__ best and highest life; __**he**__ <u>is</u> a *strengthening* and *purifying* influence like __**our**__ own mountains.

8. As the queen <u>hesitated</u> *to pass* on, young Raleigh, <u>throwing</u> __**his**__ cloak from his shoulder, <u>laid</u> __**it**__ on the miry spot, so as *to ensure* __**her**__ <u>stepping</u> over __**it**__ dryshod. *(Sir Walter Scott (1771-1832), History of Scotland)*

9. Tender-handed <u>stroke</u> a nettle,
And __**it**__ <u>stings</u> you for __**its**__ pains;
<u>Grasp</u> __**it**__ like a man of mettle,
And __**it**__ soft as silk <u>remains</u>.
(Aaron Hill (1685-1750), "Verses Written on a Window in Scotland")

10. Whatever people may <u>think</u> of __**you**__ , <u>do</u> that which __**you**__ <u>believe</u> *to be* right.

11. No man <u>is</u> so foolish but __**he**__ <u>may give</u> another good counsel sometimes, and no man so wise but __**he**__ <u>may</u> easily <u>err</u>. (Ben Jonson (1572-1637), Explorata)

III.
Answers will vary. Suggestions are given.

A young friend of mine _had_ a clever little dog, whose name _was_ Jack. He _followed_ his master whenever he _went_ to school, and always _waited_ for him until the children _finished_ . Then the dog _trotted_ along at the boy's heels until home _was_ in sight. Once some rascal _took_ Jack and _tied_ him up in a cellar a long way from home. But Jack _escaped_ and _saw_ his master again. I never _met_ a dog that _danced_ on his hind legs so gracefully as my friend's Jack.

Chapter 7: Sentences

I.
Students were instructed to make short statements about each of the persons and things given. Answers will vary. Check that they used the words properly and wrote complete sentences with proper punctuation.

Chapter 8: Sentences: Subject and Predicate

I and II.

For part one, see answers in the blanks. For part II, look for vertical line.

Answers in blanks will vary. Suggestions are given.

1. The teacher **| sat (V)** at her desk writing.
2. The captain **| marched (V)** his company in the suburbs of the town.
3. The strife **| continued (V)** with unremitting fury for three mortal hours.
4. The first permanent settlement on the Chesapeake **| was built (V)** in the beginning of the reign of James the First.
5. I **| saw (V)** an aged beggar in my walk.
6. The English army **| was (V)** too exhausted for pursuit.
7. The owls **| hooted (V)** all night long.
8. A crow **| constructed (V)** a nest in one of the young elm trees.
9. A famous man **| was named(V)** Robin Hood.
10. In the confusion, five or six of the enemy **| scattered (V)** .
11. The eyes of the savage **| glowed (V)** with fury.
12. A little leak **| sinks (V)** a great ship.
13. The blacksmith **| hammered (V)** the red-hot iron.
14. A sudden **storm (N) |** clouded the sky.
15. My **aunt (N) |** was then in London.
16. The **creature (N) |** followed us over the moor.
17. **General Washington (N) |** commanded the American army.
18. The **children (N) |** have wandered about nearly all day.
19. A high **wind (N) |** blew hats and bonnets about.
20. The **crew (N) |** fired a broadside at the enemy.
21. Many **fish (N) |** were swimming in the pool.
22. <u>Down</u> **fell (V)** <u>the timber</u> |with a crash. (*Note: This sentence is ordered differently. The subject is underlined and the predicate is double-underlined.*)
23. <u>Higher and higher</u> **climbed (V)** |<u>the sun</u>. (*Note: This sentence is ordered differently. The subject is underlined and the predicate is double-underlined.*)

Chapter 9: Complete and Simple Subject and Predicate

1. <u>She</u> | <u>roams</u> the dreary waste.
2. Ten thousand <u>warblers</u> | <u>cheer</u> the day.
3. <u>Thou</u> | <u>climbest</u> the mountain-top.
4. The <u>river</u> | <u>glideth</u> at his own sweet will.
5. The <u>rings</u> of iron | <u>sent</u> out a jarring sound.
6. The bolted <u>gates</u> | <u>flew</u> open at the blast.
7. The <u>streets</u> | <u>ring</u> with clamors.
8. The <u>courser</u> | <u>pawed</u> the ground with restless feet.
   (John Dryden (1631-1700), "Palamon and Arcite," a poem retelling the "A Knight's Tale")
9. <u>Envy</u> | <u>can</u> never <u>dwell</u> in noble hearts.
10. His whole <u>frame</u> | <u>was trembling</u>.
11. The wondering <u>stranger</u> | round him <u>gazed</u>.
    (Sir Walter Scott (1771-1832), "Lady of the Lake")

Chapter 10: The Copula (Linking Verb) "Is"

I.
1. Fishes **are** cold-blooded animals.
2. Milton **was** a great poet.
3. Washington **was** the Father of his Country.
4. You **are** studious children.
5. Thou **art** the man.
6. You **are** a studious child.
7. He **is** a colonel.

II.
Students were asked to circle the copula (linking verb). They are shown in bold below. The words connected by the copula are underlined.

1. The <u>stranger</u> **is** an <u>Austrian.</u>
2. Your <u>friends</u> **will be** <u>glad</u> to see you.
3. <u>We</u> **shall be** too <u>tired</u> to walk home.
4. <u>Seals</u> **are** amphibious <u>animals</u>.
5. <u>I</u> **am** an American <u>citizen</u>.
6. The <u>streets</u> **were** <u>wet</u> and <u>muddy</u>.
7. <u>Platinum</u> **is** a very heavy <u>metal</u>.
8. <u>Washington</u> **had been** an <u>officer</u> under Braddock.
9. The <u>Indians</u> on Cape Cod **were** <u>friendly</u>.
10. <u>We</u> **have been** <u>careless</u>.
11. <u>Sidney Lanier</u> **was** a <u>native</u> of Georgia.

Chapter 11: Interrogative Sentences, Part 1

I.

1. Check for questions about ten objects in the schoolroom.
2. Check for ten questions about some person or event famous in American history.
3. Check that the student has written answers to the questions from 1 and 2.

II.

Suggested interrogative sentences are given.

1. Does our society meet once a fortnight?
2. Who defeated Napoleon at Waterloo?
3. Did they hear the din of the battle?
4. Who wrote *Gulliver's Travels*?
5. When did Shakespeare live?
6. Was your voyage prosperous?
7. Is there anything that dries more quickly than a tear?
8. Where did Sir John Franklin perish?
9. Does the Hudson's Bay Company deal in furs?
10. Who was second President of the United States?
11. Was Victoria Empress of India?
12. Was William II the German Emperor?
13. Is Siberia a part of the Russian Empire?

III.

Do you observe any difference in the order of words? *Usually the subject is rearranged from the original.*

With what words do many questions begin? *Who, what, does, is, when, etc.*

See if you can frame a rough-and-ready rule for interrogative sentences. *Interrogative sentences ask questions and often begin with question words such as who, what, when, where, how, does, did, etc.*

Chapter 12: Interrogative Sentences, Part 2

I.
Students were instructed to write interrogative sentences.
Answers will vary. Use the examples from chapter 11 as a guide.

II.
Check for ten interrogative sentences beginning with *who, whose, whom, which,* or *what.*
Check for ten sentences answering the questions.

III.
The complete subject is underlined once; the complete predicate twice. The simple subject is marked with S; the simple predicate with V. Sometimes the verb phrase in the simple predicate is split.

1. Is **(V)**   wealth **(S)**   thy passion?
2. What shall **(V)**   I **(S)**   say **(V)** in excuse for this long letter?
3. Is **(V)**   he **(S)**   not able to pay the money?
4. Urge **(V)**   you **(S)**   your petitions in the street?
5. Why was **(V)**   James **(S)**   driven **(V)** from the throne?
6. Is **(V)**   this **(S)**   the welcome of my worthy deeds?
7. Why dost **(V)**   thou **(S)**   bend **(V)** thine eyes upon the earth?
8. Why do **(V)**   you **(S)**   treat **(V)** Alfred Burnham so defiantly?
9. Did **(V)**   you **(S)**   ever read **(V)** anything so delightful?
10. Why would **(V)** not   you **(S)**   speak **(V)** sooner?
11. Does **(V)**   this garden **(S)**   belong **(V)** to the governor?

Chapter 13: Imperative Sentences

I.

Check for ten imperative sentences. Answers will vary.

Imperative sentences give a command and usually have an implied subject *you*.

II.

Check for ten imperative sentences beginning with *do not*.

Observe that this is the common form of a prohibition (or negative command).

III.

Students were instructed to analyze the following imperative sentences.

1. <u>Go (V)</u>   you   <u>before to Gloucester with these letters.</u> (*Shakespeare (1564-1616),* King Lear)

2. <u>Follow (V)</u>   thou   <u>the flowing river.</u> (*William Wordsworth (1770-1850), "The Longest Day."*)

3. <u>Go (V)</u>   you   <u>into the other street.</u>

4. <u>(You)</u>   <u>Tomorrow in the battle think (V) on me.</u> (*William Shakespeare (1564-1616),* Richard III)

5. <u>(You)</u>   <u>Do (V) not lay (V) your hand on your sword.</u>

6. <u>(You)</u>   <u>Bring (V) forth the prisoners instantly.</u>

7. <u>(You)</u>   <u>Lend (V) favorable ears to our request.</u>

8. <u>Call (V)</u>   thou   <u>my brother hither.</u>

9. <u>(You)</u>   <u>Do (V) not seek (V) for trouble.</u>

10. <u>(You)</u>   <u>Spare (V) my guiltless wife and my poor children.</u> (*William Shakespeare (1564-1616),* Richard III)

11. <u>(You)</u>   <u>See (V) the wild waste of all-devouring years.</u> (*Alexander Pope (1688-1744),* Moral Essays)

12. <u>(You)</u>   <u>Do (V) n't measure (V) other people's corn by your own bushel.</u>

13. <u>(You)</u>   <u>Teach (V) not thy lips such scorn.</u> (*William Shakespeare (1564-1616),* Richard III)

14. <u>(You)</u>   <u>Give (V) my regards to your brother.</u>

15. <u>(You)</u>   <u>Do (V) n't forget (V) my message.</u>

16. <u>(You)</u>   <u>Remember (V) never to be ashamed of doing right.</u>

17. <u>(You)</u>   <u>Do (V) not saw (V) the air too much with your hand.</u>

18. <u>(You)</u>   <u>Keep (V) a firm rein upon these bursts of passion.</u>

19. <u>(You)</u>   <u>Do (V) not spur (V) a free horse.</u>

20. <u>(You)</u>   <u>Do (V) not stand (V) in your own light.</u>

Chapter 14: Exclamatory Sentences

Check the sentences for D, Int, Imp and E.

Int   1. Did you ever hear the streams talk to you in May, when you went a-fishing?

D   2. The white pavilions made a show,
              Like remnants of the winter snow.
              (Sir Walter Scott (1771-1832), "Marmion")

Int, E   3. But hark! what means yon faint halloo? *(Sir Walter Scott (1771-1832), "Lady of the Lake")*

D   4. Things are stagnant enough in town.
              (Lord Byron (1788-1824), Letters and Journals of Lord Byron*)*

Int   5. But what's the use of delaying?
              (William Makepeace Thackeray (1811-1863), The Book of Snobs*)*

D   6. The Moors from forth the greenwood came riding one by one.
              (John Gibson Lockhart (1794-1854), "Garci Perez de Vargas")

D   7. I was just planning a whole week's adventure for you.

D   8. At the Peckham end there were a dozen handsome trees, and under them a piece of artificial water
              where boys were sailing toy boats, and a poodle was swimming.
              (George Moore (1852-1933), Esther Waters: an English Story*)*

Imp   9. Look at the splendid prize that was to recompense our labor.

Imp   10. Don't think that my temper is hot.

D   11. The natives came by degrees to be less apprehensive of any danger from me.
              (Jonathan Swift (1667-1745), Gulliver's Travels*)*

Imp, E   12. Soldier, rest! thy warfare o'er,
              Sleep the sleep that knows not breaking.
              (Sir Walter Scott (1771-1832), "Soldier, Rest! Thy Warfare O'er")

D, E   13. How easily you seem to get interested in new people!

D, E   14. How little I thought what the quarrel would lead to!

Int   15. How have you been employing your time?

Imp   16. "O, cease your sports," Earl Percy said,
              "And take your bows with speed."
              (Author unknown, The Ballad of Chevy Chase*)*

D   17. He had been in business in the West End.

Imp   18. Abandon this mad enterprise.

Imp   19. Forgive my hasty words.

D, E   20. What black despair, what horror, fills his heart!
              (James Thomson (1700-1748), "Lost in the Snow")

Chapter 15: Vocative

I.

Answers will vary. Suggestions are given.

1. We shall miss you very much, __**Jane**__ .
2. Come hither, __**child**__ , and sit upon my knee.
3. What is your name, __**son**__ ?
4. __**Sir**__ , can you tell me the road to Denver?
5. __**Woodman**__ , spare that tree. *(George Pope Morris (1802-1864), "Woodman, Spare That Tree")*
6. Don't disappoint me, __**John**__ . I trust you absolutely.
7. Jog on, __**Lightning**__ , and we shall soon reach the stable.
8. Run, __**George**__ ! The savages are after us!
9. Swim, __**David**__ , for your life. There's a shark chasing you!
10. Jump, __**Tom**__ ! It's our last chance!

II.

Complete subjects are underlined once and complete predicates twice. Vocatives are labeled with V.

1. O learned sir, (**V**)
    You and your learning I revere.
    (William Cowper (1731-1800), "The Ninth Satire of the First Book of Horace")
2. The good old man
    Means no offense, sweet lady (**V**)!
    (Samuel Taylor Coleridge (1722-1834), Zapolya)
3. Goodbye! (You) Drive on, coachman (**V**).
4. Why, Sir John (**V**), my face does you no harm.
5. Good cousin (**V**), (You) give me audience for a while.
6. Yours is the prize, victorious prince (**V**).
7. "(You) Wake, Allan-bane (**V**)," aloud she cried
    To the old minstrel by her side.
    (Sir Walter Scott (1771-1832), "Lady of the Lake")
8. (You) Bid adieu, my sad heart (**V**), bid adieu to thy peace. *(William Cowper (1731-1800), "On Delia")*
9. My dear little cousin (**V**), what can be the matter?
10. (You) Come, Evening (**V**), once again, season of peace (**V**)! *(William Cowper (1731-1800), "Evening")*
11. Plain truth, dear Murray (**V**), needs no flowers of speech. *(Alexander Pope (1688-1744), The Sixth Epistle of the First Book of Horace, "To Mr. Murray")*
12. (You) Permit me now, Sir William (**V**), to address myself personally to you. *(Letter III to Sir William Draper from Junius, 1769)*
13. (You) Go, my dread lord (**V**), to your great-grandsire's tomb. *(William Shakespeare (1564-1616), Henry V)*
14. Why do you stay so long, my lords of France (**V**)? *(William Shakespeare, (1564-1616) Henry V)*

15. My pretty cousins (**V**), <u>you</u> <u>mistake me much</u>. (*William Shakespeare (1564-1616)*, Richard III)

16. (You) <u>Come on</u>, Lord Hastings (**V**). <u>Will</u> <u>you</u> <u>go with me</u>? (*William Shakespeare (1564-1616)*, Richard III)

17. O Romeo (**V**), Romeo (**V**), <u>brave Mercutio's</u> <u>dead</u>. (*William Shakespeare (1564-1616)*, Romeo and Juliet)
    Note: The contraction Mercutio's makes it easy to miss the verb is. *Compare, "<u>Mercutio</u> <u>is dead</u>."*

18. <u>I</u> <u>will avenge this insult</u>, noble queen (**V**). (*Alfred, Lord Tennyson (1809-1892)*, Idylls of the King)

19. O friend (**V**), <u>I</u> <u>seek a harborage for the night</u>. (*Alfred, Lord Tennyson (1809-1892)*, Idylls of the King)

20. My lord (**V**), <u>I</u> <u>saw three bandits by the rock</u>. (*Alfred, Lord Tennyson (1809-1892)*, Idylls of the King)

21. Father! (**V**) <u>thy days</u> <u>have passed in peace</u>. (*Lord Byron (1788-1824), "The Giaour"*)

III.

D   1. <u>I</u> | <u>had</u> a violent fit of the nightmare.

D   2. <u>It</u> | <u>was</u> at the time of the annual fair.

D   3. My <u>uncle</u> | <u>was</u> an old traveler.

D   4. The young <u>lady</u> | <u>closed</u> the casement with a sigh. (*Washington Irving (1783-1859)*, Tales of a Traveler)

D   5. The supper <u>table</u> | <u>was</u> at length laid.

Imp   6. (You) | <u>Hoist</u> out the boat.

Int   7. <u>Are</u> | <u>you</u> from the farm? (*Note that "from the farm" is part of the predicate.*)

D   8. <u>She</u> | <u>broke</u> into a little scornful laugh. (*Alfred, Lord Tennyson (1809-1892)*, Idylls of the King)

Imp   9. (You) | <u>Bring</u> forth the horse.

Int   10. When <u>can</u> their <u>glory</u> | <u>fade</u>? (*Alfred, Lord Tennyson (1809-1892), "Charge of the Light Brigade"*)

Imp,E   11. (You) | <u>Shut, shut</u> the door, good John (V)! (*Alexander Pope (1688-1744), "Epistle to Dr. Arbuthnot"*)
    Note: Exclamatory sentences can be declarative, imperative, or interrogative as well as exclamatory. Students should note both when they encounter an exclamatory sentence.

Int   12. <u>Do you</u> | <u>mark</u> that, my lord (V)?

Int   13. Why <u>sigh</u> | <u>you</u> so profoundly? (*Note that the subject "you" is surrounded by the predicate.*)

D   14. Within the mind strong <u>fancies</u> | <u>work</u>. (*William Wordsworth (1770-1850), "The Pass of Kirkstone"*)

D   15. The <u>sun</u> | <u>peeps</u> gay at dawn of day. (*William Allingham (1824-1889), "The Bird"*)

D   16. The noble <u>stag</u> | <u>was pausing</u> now
    Upon the mountain's southern brow.
    (*Sir Walter Scott (1771-1832), "Lady of the Lake"*)

D   17. Then through the dell his <u>horn</u> | <u>resounds</u>. (*Sir Walter Scott (1771-1832), "The Stag Hunt"*)

D   18. Lightly and brightly <u>breaks</u> away
    The <u>Morning</u> from her mantle gray.
    (*Lord Byron (1788-1824), "The Assault"*)

D   19. <u>Fire</u> | <u>flashed</u> from out the old Moor's eyes. (*Lord Byron (1788-1824), "Siege and Conquest of Alhama"*)

D   20. The <u>garlands</u> | <u>wither</u> on their brow. (*James Shirley (1596-1666), "Death the Leveller"*)

IV.

Note that students may form questions differently from these suggestions.

What changes do you make in the form of each sentence? *The sentence order is altered and sometimes a question word is added.*

1. Did I have a violent fit of the nightmare?
2. Was it at the time of the annual fair?
3. Was my uncle an old traveler?
4. Did the young lady close the casement with a sigh?
5. Was the supper table at length laid?
6. Did you hoist out the boat?
7. (Already interrogative)
8. Did she break into a little scornful laugh?
9. Did you bring forth the horse?
10. (Already interrogative)
11. Did you shut the door?
12. (Already interrogative)
13. (Already interrogative)
14. Do strong fancies work within the mind?
15. Does the sun peep gay at dawn of day?
16. Was the noble stag pausing now
    Upon the mountain's southern brow?
17. Does his horn resound through the dell?
18. Does the Morning break away lightly and brightly from her mantle gray?
19. Did the fire flash from out the old Moor's eyes?
20. Do the garlands wither on their brow?

Chapter 16: Adjectives

I.
Students were asked to circle the adjectives. They are in bold print here. They were to draw an arrow to the noun or pronoun that it modifies. It is underlined here. *Note: Possessive pronouns serve as adjectives, but they are not identified here. Likewise, prepositional phrases serving as adjectives (such as "of this vessel" in #8) are not labeled since students have not studied prepositional phrases yet.*

1. The <u>sun</u> is **warm**, the <u>sky</u> is **clear**. *(Percy Bysshe Shelley (1792-1822), "Stanzas Written in Dejection, Near Naples")*
2. Hope must have **green** <u>bowers</u> and **blue** <u>skies</u>. *(Thomas Hood (1799-1845), "The Plea of the Midsummer Fairies")*
3. His <u>axe</u> is **keen**, his <u>arm</u> is **strong**. *(Thomas Hood (1799-1845), "The Elm Tree")*
4. La Fleur instantly pulled out a **little dirty** <u>pocket-book</u>, crammed full of **small** <u>letters</u>. *(Laurence Sterne (1713-1768), Sentimental Journey Through France and Italy)*
5. His **white** <u>hair</u> floats like a snowdrift around his face. *(Nathaniel Hawthorne (1804-1864), "P's Correspondence")*
6. A **sorrowful** <u>multitude</u> followed them to the shore. *(Nathaniel Hawthorne (1804-1864), Tanglewood Tales)*
7. My **fugitive** <u>years</u> are all hasting away. *(William Cowper (1731-1800), "The Poplar Field")*
8. The <u>sails</u> of this vessel are **black**. *(Nathaniel Hawthorne (1804-1864), Tanglewood Tales)*
9. The **old** <u>officer</u> was reading a **small** <u>pamphlet</u>. *(Laurence Sterne (1713-1768), Sentimental Journey Through France and Italy)*
10. <u>He</u> was almost **frantic** with grief.
11. <u>We</u> are **weak** and **miserable**. *(John Calvin (1509-1564), from a sermon)*
12. A more **striking** <u>picture</u> there could not be imagined than the **beautiful English** <u>face</u> of the girl, and its **exquisite** <u>bloom</u>, together with her **erect** and **independent** <u>attitude</u>, contrasted with the **sallow** and **bilious** <u>skin</u> of the Malay, veneered with **mahogany** <u>tints</u> by climate and **marine** <u>air</u>, his **small, fierce, restless** <u>eyes</u>, **thin** <u>lips</u>, **slavish** <u>gestures</u> and <u>adorations</u>. *(Thomas De Quincey (1785-1859), Confessions of an English Opium-Eater)*

II.
Answers will vary. Suggestions are given.

1. A __**stone**__ palace rose before us.
2. A __**dusty**__ path led down to the brook.
3. __**Vengeful**__ Indians attacked the village.
4. The __**brave**__ soldier was severely wounded.
5. __**Unruly**__ boys threw stones at the train.
6. A __**lone**__ lamp was burning in the room.
7. A __**tall**__ tower stood on the cliff.
8. Two __**fierce**__ dogs guarded the house.
9. The __**absent-minded**__ pupil has forgotten his book.
10. __**High**__ walls surrounded the garden.
11. The __**angry**__ elephant seized his tormentor.
12. This __**enterprising**__ merchant lived in Chicago.

III.

Answers will vary. Suggestions are given.

1. A fierce **thief** sprang at the beggar.
2. Envious **men** are never happy.
3. The cowardly **man** deserted his companion.
4. A heavy **weight** fell from the staging.
5. A bright **fire** blazed on the hearth.
6. Smooth **stones** covered the sidewalk.
7. A golden **crown** was on his head.
8. Many **hands** make light work.
9. My faithful **friend** never left me.
10. Dark **clouds** shut out the sun.
11. A cold **wind** is blowing.
12. The tall **tree** was covered with snow.
13. A soft **answer** turneth away wrath.
14. Angry **men** seldom give good advice.
15. Four black **horses** drew the coach.

Chapter 17: Classes of Adjectives

I.

Students were instructed to fill in the blanks with adjectives. Answers will vary. Suggestions are given.

1. Spring is cheery, but winter is __dreary__. *(Thomas Hood (1799-1845), "Ballad")*
2. A __little__ fairy comes at night. Her eyes are __blue__, her hair is __brown__. *(Thomas Hood (1799-1845), "The Dream Fairy")*
3. The __glorious__ castle had never held half so many __noble__ knights beneath its roof.
4. Holly is __green__ in the winter.
5. No __warm__ fire blazed on the hearth.
6. Wellington was an __amazing__ general.
7. I wish you a __happy__ New Year.
8. Down he sank in the __crashing__ waves.
9. The clothes and food of the children are __new__ and __fresh__.
10. His eyes are __red__ with weeping.
11. "'Twas a __narrow__ victory," said the __tired__ man.
12. __Glistening__ snow lay on the ground.
13. No footstep marked the __small__ gravel.
14. Miss Bell seemed very __kind__.
15. John looks as __proper__ as a judge.

II.

Check for twenty sentences using the listed adjectives with a noun. Answers will vary.

III.

Answers will vary. Suggestions are given.

1. iron: *black, course, hard, red-hot*
2. lead: *gray, shiny, heavy*
3. robin: *sweet, happy, red-breasted*
4. parrot: *loud, funny, colorful*
5. eagle: *majestic, proud, big*
6. sparrow: *tiny, small, soft*
7. bicycle: *shiny, red, new*
8. horse: *tall, fast, gentle*
9. oxen: *giant, quiet, tired*
10. cornfield: *green, bountiful, lush*
11. spring: *sweet-smelling, warm, flowery*
12. summer: *long, hot, sticky*
13. autumn: *crisp, chilly, dry*
14. winter: *cold, quiet, snow-covered*
15. butterfly: *light, winged, colorful*
16. spider: *black, creepy, delicate*
17. carpenter: *careful, kind, dusty*
18. physician: *friendly, smart, kind*
19. sugar: *sweet, crunchy, white*

20. marble: *shiny, smooth, hard*

IV.

Students were instructed to write sentences using the words provided. Check that the adjectives were used correctly in complete sentences. Answers will vary.

Chapter 18: The Two Articles

I.
Students were instructed to underline indefinite articles.

1. Whenever there was sickness in the place, she was **an** untiring nurse. *(Thomas Hughes (1822-1896), Tom Brown at Oxford)*

2. We are going to have **a** great archery party next month, and you shall have **an** invitation. *(Thomas Hughes (1822-1896), Tom Brown at Oxford)*

3. But man of all ages is **a** selfish animal, and unreasonable in his selfishness. *(Thomas Hughes (1822-1896), Tom Brown at Oxford)*

4. There is **a** pleasure in the pathless woods. *(Lord Byron (1788-1824), "There is a Pleasure in the Pathless Woods")*

5. At length I met **a** reverend good old man. *(George Herbert (1593-1632), "Peace")*

6. He was lying on **a** crimson velvet sofa, reading **a** French novel. It was **a** very little book. He is **a** very little man. In that enormous hall he looked like **a** mere speck. *(William Makepeace Thackeray (1811-1863), The Book of Snobs)*

II.
Check that students have properly filled in blanks with the correct definite or indefinite article. All of the following sentences are taken from "The Legend of Sleepy Hollow" by Washington Irving (1783-1859).

1. The schoolhouse was __a__ low building rudely constructed of logs; __the__ windows were partly glazed, and partly patched with leaves of old copybooks.

2. He was always ready for either __a__ fight or __a__ frolic.

3. It was, as I have said, __a__ fine autumnal day. __The__ sky was clear and serene.

4. __A__ sloop was loitering in __the__ distance, dropping slowly down with __the__ tide, her sail hanging uselessly against __the__ mast.

5. __The__ musician was __an__ old gray-headed negro.

6. On one side of __the__ church extends a wide woody dell, along which raves __a__ large brook.

III.
Students were told to label the definite articles with a D and the indefinite with an I and draw an arrow to the noun to which it belongs. The noun is underlined here.

1. **An (I)** acquaintance, **a (I)** friend as he called himself, entered.

2. **The (D)** town was in **a (I)** hubbub.

3. **The (D)** men were quiet and sober.

4. You see this man about whom so great **an (I)** uproar hath been made in this town. *(John Bunyan (1628-1688), The Pilgrim's Progress)*

5. I disliked carrying **a (I)** musket. *(Oliver Goldsmith (1730-1774), "Essays")*

6. I sat down on one of **the (D)** benches, at **the (D)** other end of which was seated **a (I)** man in very shabby clothes. *(Oliver Goldsmith (1730-1774), "The Strolling Player")*

7. **The (D)** ploughman whistles. *(John Milton (1608-1674), "L'Allegro")*

8. **The (D)** mower whets his scythe. *(Oscar Wilde (1854-1900), "The Burden of Itys")*

9. Young and old come forth to play
   On **a** (**I**) sunshine <u>holiday</u>.
   (John Milton (1608-1674), "L'Allegro")

Chapter 19: Adverbs

I.
Students were instructed to circle the adverbs and underline the verb or verb phrase twice. Adverbs are bolded below. The student should have drawn an arrow from the adverb to the verb. *Note: Prepositional phrases that serve as adverbs, such as "in the air" in #1, are not labeled since students have not studied prepositional phrases yet.*

1. Carroll <u>waved</u> his whip **triumphantly** in the air.
2. This contemptuous speech **cruelly** <u>shocked</u> Cecilia. *(Fanny Burney (1752-1840), Cecilia: Or Memoirs of an Heiress)*
3. Spring <u>came</u> upon us **suddenly**.
4. The king <u>gained</u> ground **everywhere**.
5. Every night in dreams they <u>groaned</u> **aloud**.
6. **Northward** he <u>turneth</u> through a little door.
7. I **dimly** <u>discerned</u> a wall before me.
8. Miss Sharp had **demurely** <u>entered</u> the carriage some minutes before. *(William Makepeace Thackeray (1811-1863), Vanity Fair)*
9. Punctuality at meals <u>was</u> **rigidly** <u>enforced</u> at Gateshead Hall. *(Charlotte Brontë (1816-1855), Jane Eyre)*
10. But here the doctors **eagerly** <u>dispute</u>.
11. The guardsman <u>defended</u> himself **bravely**.
12. **Swiftly, swiftly** <u>flew</u> the ship,
    Yet she <u>sailed</u> **softly** too:
    Sweetly, sweetly <u>blew</u> the breeze —
    On me alone it <u>blew</u>.
    (Samuel Taylor Coleridge (1722-1834), "The Rime of the Ancient Mariner")
13. Kent <u>had been looking</u> at me **steadily** for some time.
14. By this storm our ship <u>was</u> **greatly** <u>damaged</u>.

II.
Answers will vary. Check to be sure the sentences were done correctly.

III.
Fill in each blank with an adverb (suggestions given) and tell what it modifies (modified word shown in bold).

1. This poor fellow has been _badly_ **hurt**.
2. All the pupils were _quite_ **delighted** with the entertainment.
3. The explosion did _unbelievably_ **great** damage.
4. Joe **passed** his hand _slowly_ over his aching forehead.
5. The prisoner **struggled** _mightily_ .
6. _So_ **many** objections were heard.
7. I am not _very_ **unhappy**, but still I am _quite_ **uncomfortable**.

8. Helen speaks _quite_ **rapidly**; John does not speak **rapidly** _much_ .
9. The wind **howled** _swiftly_ down the wide chimney.
10. My boat **will hold** six persons _comfortably_ .
11. The room is not **large** _enough_ for the class.
12. The scout **crept** _stealthily_ through the thicket.
13. Jackson's salary is _too_ **small** for his needs.
14. The river is **rising** _up_ rapidly.
15. Such conduct **will be** _swiftly_ **punished**.

Chapter 20: Adverbs Modifying Adjectives

Students were instructed to circle the adverbs that modify adjectives (bolded below) and draw an arrow to the adjective it modifies (underlined).

1. Her language is **singularly** agreeable to me. (*Charlotte Brontë (1816-1855)*, Jane Eyre)
2. Mr. Sedley's eyes twinkled in a manner **indescribably** roguish. (*William Makepeace Thackeray (1811-1863)*, Vanity Fair)
3. The river walk is **uncommonly** pretty.
4. She had been going on a **bitterly** cold winter night to visit some one at Stamford Hill. (*William Black (1841-1898)*, Kilmeny)
5. Mrs. Harrel was **extremely** uneasy.
6. The meeting was **very** painful to them both.
7. Kate had been **unreasonably** angry with Heatherleigh.
8. Be **particularly** careful not to stumble.
9. The poor fellow was **pitifully** weak.

Chapter 21: Adverbs Modifying Adverbs

Students were instructed to circle the adverbs that modify other adverbs (bolded below) and draw an arrow to the adverb it modifies (underlined).

1. She told her distress **quite** frankly.
2. Cecilia then **very** gravely began an attempt to undeceive her. (*Fanny Burney (1752-1840)*, Cecilia: Or Memoirs of an Heiress)
3. This service she **somewhat** reluctantly accepted.
4. He fixed his eyes on me **very** steadily. (*Charlotte Brontë (1816-1855)*, Jane Eyre)
5. We strolled along **rather** carelessly towards Hampstead.
6. Do not speak **so** indistinctly.
7. The red horse trots **uncommonly** fast.
8. The commander rebuked his boldness **half** seriously, **half** jestingly.
9. The cotton must be picked **pretty** soon.
10. Why did King Lear's daughters treat him **so** unkindly?

Chapter 22: Classification of Adverbs

I.

Suggested adverbs of degree are given. Answers will vary.

1. The wind blew __so__ hard.
2. The air bites shrewdly; it is __very__ cold.
3. I was in the utmost astonishment, and roared __so__ loud that they all ran back in fright.
4. I bowed __exceedingly__ respectfully to the governor.
5. The peacock's voice is not __so__ beautiful as his plumage.
6. We jogged homeward merrily __enough__. *(Lord Byron (1788-1824), Letters and Journals of Lord Byron)*
7. Tom was __too__ angry to measure his words.
8. The load was __much__ too heavy for the horse to draw.
9. "My lesson is __very__ hard. Is yours?" "No, not very; but still it is __somewhat__ difficult."
10. The physician was rather surprised to find his patient __so__ lively.
11. This has been an __exceptionally__ dry season.

II.

Students should form adverbs from the list of words. Sentences will vary. Check for completeness and sense.

1.	fine	**finely**
2.	courageous	**courageously**
3.	brave	**bravely**
4.	splendid	**splendidly**
5.	eager	**eagerly**
6.	plain	**plainly**
7.	doubtful	**doubtfully**
8.	confusing	**confusingly**
9.	remarkable	**remarkably**
10.	heedless	**heedlessly**
11.	careful	**carefully**
12.	polite	**politely**
13.	rude	**rudely**
14.	civil	**civilly**
15.	violent	**violently**
16.	mild	**mildly**
17.	meek	**meekly**
18.	gentle	**gently**
19.	smooth	**smoothly**
20.	soft	**softly**
21.	boisterous	**boisterously**

III.

Answers will vary.

IV.

Students were asked to use each of the following verbs and verb phrases with several different adverbs, and see how the meaning varies. Answers will vary. Suggestions are given.

1. sings: **happily, woefully, loudly, softly**
2. runs: **slowly, fast, haltingly, gracefully**
3. flies: **high, low, lightly, heavily**
4. talks: **quietly, loudly, rudely, harshly**
5. walks: **quickly, stealthily, awkwardly**
6. works: **hard, lazily, slowly, efficiently**
7. acted: **carelessly, generously, kindly, hurtfully**
8. spent: **carefully, excessively, frugally, wastefully**
9. played: **correctly, incorrectly, fairly, unfairly**
10. rushes: **quickly, hurriedly, rudely, carelessly**
11. has confessed: **honestly, kindly, humbly, pridefully**
12. were marching: **proudly, loudly, slowly, defiantly**
13. are writing: **neatly, sloppily, hurriedly, carefully**
14. gazed: **lovingly, proudly, thoughtfully, sweetly**
15. have examined: **carefully, gently, quickly, cautiously**
16. will study: **deeply, slowly, thoughtfully, carelessly**
17. devoured: **hungrily, greedily, quickly, hurriedly**
18. shall watch: **carefully, jealously, carelessly, casually**
19. may hurt: **deeply, barely, nearly, totally**
20. can ride: **slowly, quickly, thankfully, freely**
21. has injured: **completely, partially, slightly, totally**
22. will attack: **violently, quietly, bloodlessly, loudly**

V.

Complete this exercise orally with your student.

VI.

Students were instructed to pick out all the adverbs in chapter 19, Exercises I and II and tell whether they are adverbs of time, place, manner, or degree, and indicate what verb, adjective, or adverb each modifies.

Chapter 19, I

1. manner; waved
2. manner; shocked
3. time; came
4. place; gained
5. manner; groaned
6. place; turneth
7. degree (or manner); discerned
8. manner; entered
9. manner; was enforced
10. manner; dispute
11. manner; defended
12. manner; flew
    manner; sailed
    manner; blew

13. manner; had been looking
14. degree; was damaged

<u>Chapter 19, II</u>
1. manner; laughed
2. manner; sang
3. manner; have acted
4. manner; settled
5. manner; made
6. time; rowed
7. manner; entered
8. manner; waited

VII.
Answers will vary.

Chapter 23: Analysis: Modifiers

I.

Students were instructed to analyze the sentences below.

Note: The prepositional phrases are shown in parentheses. Students have not yet been introduced to prepositional phrases, so they do not need to label them at all. If your student does label them and tries to identify them, they are marked here as adjective or adverbial phrases.

1. The (**Adj**) large (**Adj**) <u>room</u> | <u>was</u> quickly (**Adv**) <u>filled</u>.

2. A (**Adj**) great (**Adj**) wood (**Adj**) <u>fire</u> | <u>blazed</u> cheerfully (**Adv**).

3. Our (**Adj**) dusty (**Adj**) <u>battalions</u> | <u>marched</u> onward (**Adv**).

4. The (**Adj**) heavy (**Adj**) <u>gates</u> | <u>were shut</u> instantly (**Adv**).

5. A (**Adj**) magnificent (**Adj**) snow-fed (**Adj**) <u>river</u> | <u>poured</u> ceaselessly (**Adv**) (through the glen) (**Adv**).

6. Back (**Adv**) <u>darted</u> | <u>Spurius Lartius</u>.

7. A (**Adj**) meager (**Adj**) little (**Adj**) <u>man</u> | <u>was standing</u> near (**Adv**).

8. This (**Adj**) terrible (**Adj**) <u>winter</u> | <u>dragged</u> slowly (**Adv**) along (**Adv**).

9. The (**Adj**) <u>cattle</u> | <u>were feeding</u> quietly (**Adv**).

10. Instantly (**Adv**) a (**Adj**) dire (**Adj**) <u>hubbub</u> | <u>arose</u>.

11. The (**Adj**) red (**Adj**) <u>sun</u> | <u>sank</u> slowly (**Adv**) (behind the hills) (**Adv**).

12. Many (**Adj**) strange (**Adj**) <u>stories</u> | <u>were told</u> (of this adventure) (**Adj modifying** *stories*).

II.

Students were instructed to expand the following short sentences by inserting modifiers of the subject and of the predicate. Answers will vary. The first one is suggested for you.

1. Men work. ***Strong men work diligently.***

Chapter 24: Prepositions

I.
Suggested prepositions are shown in the blanks below.

1. John's hat *hung* __on__ the *peg*.
2. The river *rises* __in__ the *mountains* and *flows* __across__ a great *plain* __to__ the *sea*.
3. The miseries of numbed hands and shivering skins no longer accompany every *pull* __on__ the river. *(Thomas Hughes (1822-1896),* Tom Brown at Oxford*)*
4. He *was* __in__ a particularly *good-humor* with himself.
5. His conscience pricked him for *intruding* __on__ *Hardy* during his hours of work. *(Thomas Hughes (1822-1896),* Tom Brown at Oxford*)*
6. Tom came to understand the *differences* __in__ his two *heroes*. *(Thomas Hughes (1822-1896),* Tom Brown at Oxford*)*
7. Such cruelty *fills* us __with__ *indignation*.
8. He was *haunted* __by__ a hundred *fears*.
9. __In__ a score of *minutes* Garbetts *came* back __with__ an anxious and crestfallen *countenance*. *(William Makepeace Thackeray (1811-1863),* History of Pendennis*)*
10. To *drive* the deer __with__ *hound* and *horn*
    Earl Percy took his way.
    (Author unknown, The Ballad of Chevy Chase*)*
11. Cooks, butlers, and their assistants were *bestirring* themselves __in__ the *kitchen*. *(Thomas Hughes (1822-1896),* Tom Brown at Oxford*)*
12. The weary traveler *was sleeping* __under__ a *tree*.
13. Jack *hid* __behind__ the *door*.
14. I will *call* __after__ *dinner*.

II.
Students were asked to use prepositions in sentences. Answers will vary.

III.
Students were instructed to circle the prepositions (shown in bold); draw an arrow to their objects (shown in parentheses); underline the word(s) with which each preposition connects its object; and label the underlined word(s) with P if it is a pronoun, A if it is an article or Adj for other adjectives.

1. The village maid steals **through** the (A) (shade). *(Sir Walter Scott (1771-1832), "The Hour of Love")*
2. His eyes burnt **like** (coals) **under** his (P) deep (Adj) (brows). *(Thomas Hughes (1822-1896),* Tom Brown at Oxford*)*
3. Their vessels were moored **in** our (P) (bay). *(William Makepeace Thackeray (1811-1863),* The Chronicle of the Drum*)*
4. The hounds ran swiftly **through** the (A) (woods). *(Author unknown,* The Ballad of Chevy Chase*)*
5. They knocked **at** our (P) (gates) **for** (admittance). *(William Makepeace Thackeray (1811-1863),* The Chronicle of the Drum*)*
6. I grew weary **of** the (A) (sea) and intended to stay **at** (home) **with** my (P) (wife and family).

7. Several officers **of** <u>the **(A)**</u> (army) went **to** <u>the **(A)**</u> (door) **of** <u>the **(A)**</u> great (Adj) council (Adj) (chamber).

8. This seems **to** (me) but melancholy work. *(Thomas Carlyle (1795-1881), "Lectures on Heroes")*

9. The bowmen mustered **on** <u>the **(A)**</u> (hills). *(Author unknown, The Ballad of Chevy Chase)*

10. Death lays his icy hand **on** (kings). *(James Shirley (1596-1666), "Death the Leveller")*

11. Untie these bands from **off** <u>my **(P)**</u> (hands). *(Robert Burns (1759-1796), "McPherson's Farewell")*

12. **Down** <u>the **(A)**</u> wide **(Adj)** (stairs) a darkling way they found. *(John Keats (1795-1821), "The Eve of St. Agnes")*

13. He halts, and searches **with** <u>his **(P)**</u> (eyes)
    Among <u>the **(A)**</u> scattered **(Adj)** (rocks). *(William Wordsworth (1770-1850), "Fidelity")*

14. The cottage windows **through** <u>the **(A)**</u> (twilight) blazed. *(William Wordsworth (1770-1850), "Skating")*

15. All shod **with** (steel),
    We hissed **along** <u>the **(A)**</u> polished **(Adj)** (ice).
    (William Wordsworth (1770-1850), "Skating")

16. He was full **of** (joke and jest).

17. Lady Waldegrave swept her fingers **over** <u>a **(A)**</u> (harp) which stood near. *(Susan Ferrier (1782-1854), Destiny)*

IV.
Students were instructed to underline fifteen prepositions and circle the objects of the preposition in a poem of their choice, or in "Lochinvar," by Sir Walter Scott (1771-1832). Objects are shown in bold print.

OH! young Lochinvar is come out <u>of</u> the **west**,
<u>Through</u> all the wide **Border** his steed was the best;
And save his good broadsword he weapons had none.
He rode all unarmed and he rode all alone.
So faithful <u>in</u> **love** and so dauntless <u>in</u> **war**,
There never was knight <u>like</u> the young **Lochinvar**.

He stayed not <u>for</u> **brake** and he stopped not <u>for</u> **stone**,
He swam the Eske river where ford there was none,
But ere he alighted <u>at</u> Netherby **gate**
The bride had consented, the gallant came late:
For a laggard <u>in</u> **love** and a dastard <u>in</u> **war**
Was to wed the fair Ellen <u>of</u> brave **Lochinvar**.

So boldly he entered the Netherby Hall,
<u>Among</u> **bridesmen**, and **kinsmen**, and **brothers**, and **all**:
Then spoke the bride's father, his hand <u>on</u> his **sword**,—
<u>For</u> the poor craven **bridegroom** said never a word,—
'Oh! come ye <u>in</u> **peace** here, or come ye <u>in</u> **war**,
Or to dance <u>at</u> our **bridal**, young Lord Lochinvar?'—

'I long wooed your daughter, my suit you denied;
Love swells <u>like</u> the **Solway**, but ebbs <u>like</u> its **tide**—
And now am I come, <u>with</u> this lost **love** <u>of</u> **mine**,
To lead but one measure, drink one cup <u>of</u> **wine**.
There are maidens <u>in</u> **Scotland** more lovely <u>by</u> **far**,
That would gladly be bride <u>to</u> the young **Lochinvar**.'

The bride kissed the goblet; the knight took it up,
He quaffed <u>off</u> the **wine**, and he threw <u>down</u> the **cup**,
She looked down to blush, and she looked up to sigh,
With a smile <u>on</u> her **lips** and a tear <u>in</u> her **eye**.
He took her soft hand ere her mother could bar,—
'Now tread we a measure!' said young Lochinvar.

So stately his form, and so lovely her face,
That never a hall such a galliard did grace;
While her mother did fret, and her father did fume,
And the bridegroom stood dangling his bonnet and plume;
And the bride-maidens whispered ''Twere better <u>by</u> **far**
To have matched our fair cousin <u>with</u> young **Lochinvar**.'

One touch <u>to</u> her **hand** and one word <u>in</u> her **ear**,
When they reached the hall-door, and the charger stood near;
So light <u>to</u> the **croupe** the fair lady he swung,
So light <u>to</u> the **saddle** <u>before</u> **her** he sprung!
'She is won! we are gone, <u>over</u> **bank**, **bush**, and **scaur**;
They'll have fleet steeds that follow,' quoth young Lochinvar.

There was mounting <u>'mong</u> **Graemes** <u>of</u> the Netherby **clan**;
Fosters, Fenwicks, and Musgraves, they rode and they ran:
There was racing and chasing <u>on</u> **Cannobie Lee**,
But the lost bride <u>of</u> **Netherby** ne'er did they see.
So daring <u>in</u> **love** and so dauntless <u>in</u> **war**,
Have ye e'er heard <u>of</u> **gallant** <u>like</u> young **Lochinvar**?

Chapter 25: Conjunctions

I.
Students were instructed to circle the conjunctions (shown in bold), and place parentheses around the words, or groups of words, they connect. Note that students should carefully circle only the words connected by the conjunction. Careful work here will help them as they learn to identify compound subjects and predicates, as well as compound and complex sentences in lessons to come.

1. (The wind was high) **and** (the clouds were dark),
   And (the boat returned no more.) *(Thomas Moore (1779-1852), "A Ballad: The Lake of the Dismal Swamp")*

2. It was the time when (lilies blow),
   And (clouds are highest up in air.) *(Alfred, Lord Tennyson (1809-1892), "Lady Clare")*

3. (Beating heart) **and** (burning brow), ye are very patient now. *(Elizabeth Barrett Browning (1806-1861), "Rhyme of the Duchess May")*

4. The uncouth person in the tattered garments (dropped on both knees on the pavement), **and** (took her hand in his), **and** (kissed it in passionate gratitude.) *(William Black (1841-1898), Sunrise)*

5. He (rose), **and** (stood with his cap in his hand).

6. She (bowed to him), **and** (passed on), (grave) **and** (stately) *(William Black (1841-1898), Sunrise)*

7. She was (an amiable) **but** (strictly matter-of-fact) person. *(William Black (1841-1898), Sunrise)*

8. (Brand became (more) **and** (more) convinced) **that** (this family was the most delightful family in England). *(William Black (1841-1898), Sunrise)*

9. **If** (there were any stranger here at all), (we should not dream of asking you to sing).

10. Helen (was on the lookout for this expected guest), **and** (saw him from her window.) **But** (she did not come forward). *(William Makepeace Thackeray (1811-1863), History of Pendennis)*

11. I am (busy) **and** (content).

12. Carrying this fateful letter in his hand, he went (downstairs) **and** (out into the cool night air). *(William Black (1841-1898), Sunrise)*

13. For Romans in Rome's quarrel
    Spared **neither** (land) **nor** (gold),
    Nor (son) **nor** (wife), **nor** (limb) **nor** (life),
    In the brave days of old.
    (Lord Thomas Macaulay (1800-1859), "Horatius at the Bridge")

14. He was **neither** (angry) **nor** (impatient).

15. There were forty craft in Avès that were both (swift) **and** (stout). *(Charles Kingsley (1819-1875), "The Last Buccaneer")*

16. We knew you must come by (sooner) **or** (later).

17. (He continued his story), **though** (his listener seemed (singularly preoccupied) **and** (thoughtful.)) *(William Black (1841-1898), Sunrise)*

II. and III.
Students were instructed to compose sentences with given conjunctions. Be sure that each conjunction is used in a sentence. Answers will vary.

IV.

Students were asked to find ten conjunctions in chapter 5, Exercise I, and tell what each conjunction connects. chapter 5, Exercise I is reproduced below. Conjunctions are bolded and the words connected are shown in parentheses.

1. Goneril, the elder, (declared) **that** (she loved her father more than words could give out), **that** (he was dearer to her than the light of her own eyes). (*Adapted from Charles and Mary Lamb's* Tales from Shakespeare. *Goneril is the eldest daughter of Shakespeare's* King Lear.)

2. Bassanio (took the ring) **and** (vowed never to part with it). (*Adapted from Charles and Mary Lamb's* Tales from Shakespeare. *Bassanio is a character in Shakespeare's* Merchant of Venice.)

3. The floor of the cave (was (dry) **and** (level)), **and** (had a sort of small loose gravel upon it). (*Daniel Defoe (1660-1731), Robinson Crusoe*)

4. (Having now brought all my things on shore), **and** (secured them), I (went back to my boat), **and** (rowed), **or** (paddled her) along the shore, to her old harbor, where I laid her up. (*Daniel Defoe (1660-1731), Robinson Crusoe*)

5. Heaven lies about us in our infancy. **no conjunction** (*William Wordsworth (1770-1850), "Ode"*)

6. Blessed is he who has found his work. **no conjunction** (*Thomas Carlyle (1795-1881), "The Modern Worker"*)

7. In fact, Tom declared it was of no use to work on his farm; it was the most pestilent little piece of ground in the whole country; everything about it (went wrong), **and** (would go wrong), in spite of him. (*Washington Irving (1783-1859), "Rip Van Winkle"*)

8. When Portia parted with her husband, she (spoke cheeringly to him), **and** (bade him bring his dear friend along with him when he returned). (*Adapted from Charles and Mary Lamb's* Tales from Shakespeare. *Portia is a character in Shakespeare's* Merchant of Venice.)

V.

Fill in each blank with a conjunction. Answers will vary. Suggestions are given.

1. Iron, lead, __and__ gold are metals.
2. __Neither__ Jack nor Joe is at school.
3. __If__ you do not hurry, you will miss the train.
4. Either Mary __or__ Francis is to blame.
5. There are __either__ lions __or__ tigers in the jungle.
6. __Either__ one or the other of us must give way.

Chapter 26: Interjections

I.

Students were instructed to circle the interjections (bolded below) and write on the blank what emotion they think it expresses. Answers will vary. Suggestions are given.

1. **Fie, fie!** they are not to be named, my lord. *anger, passion*
   (*William Shakespeare (1564-1616),* Much Ado About Nothing)

2. **Pish** for thee, Iceland dog! *anger, annoyance*
   (*William Shakespeare (1564-1616),* Henry V)

3. **Lo!** where the giant on the mountain stands. *wonder, excitement*
   (*Lord Byron (1788-1824), "Childe Harold's Pilgrimage"*)

4. "**Ah me!**" she cries, "was ever moonlight seen so clear?" *wonder, amazement*
   (*Thomas Hood (1799-1845), "The Plea of the Midsummer Fairies"*)

5. **Pshaw!** this neglect is accident, and the effect of hurry. *frustration, annoyance*

6. **O,** let us yet be merciful. *honor, wonder*
   (*William Shakespeare (1564-1616),* Henry V)

7. That I did love thee, Caesar, **O,** 't is true. *passion, love*
   (*William Shakespeare (1564-1616),* Julius Caesar)

8. The Wildgrave winds his bugle-horn.
   To horse, to horse! **halloo! halloo!** *announcing, calling, excitement*
   (*Sir Walter Scott (1771-1832), "The Wild Huntsman"*)

9. **But psha!** I've the heart of a soldier, *determination, declaring*
   All gentleness, mercy, and pity.
   (*William Makepeace Thackeray (1811-1863), "The Chronicle of the Drum"*)

10. Louder rang the Wildgrave's horn,
    "Hark forward, forward! **holla, ho!**" *determination, eagerness*
    (*William Makepeace Thackeray (1811-1863), "The Chronicle of the Drum"*)

11. **Huzza for the Arethusa!** She is a frigate tight and brave. *happy, proud*
    (*Prince Hoare (1755-1834), "The Arethusa"*)

II.

Check sentences and make sure that they all include an interjection and that the student has written the emotion it expresses.

Chapter 27: Phrases

I.

Check the students sentences, making sure that they have written complete sentences and properly used the phrase. Answers will vary.

II.

Check that they student has properly identified how they used each phrase in their sentences. Was it the subject? object? adjective? adverb? Students may have difficulty identifying the part of speech. You may wish to do this together or orally.

III.

The part of speech of each word is identified below.

1. baseball club_____ *baseball: adjective   club: noun*
2. Queen (**noun**) of (**preposition**) England (**noun; object of the preposition**)
3. will (**auxiliary verb/helping verb**) come (**verb**)
4. has (**auxiliary verb/helping verb**) traveled (**verb**)
5. North American (**adjective**) Continent (**noun**)
6. Isthmus (**noun**) of (**preposition**) Suez (**noun; object of the preposition**)
7. in (**preposition**) the (**article**) street (**noun; object of the preposition**)
8. on (**preposition**) the (**article**) playground (**noun; object of the preposition**)
9. with (**preposition**) an (**article**) effort (**noun; object of the preposition**)
10. of (**preposition**) fur (**noun; object of the preposition**)
11. of (**preposition**) silver (**noun; object of the preposition**)
12. had (**auxiliary verb/helping verb**) tried (**verb**)
13. at (**preposition**) sea (**noun; object of the preposition**)
14. at (**preposition**) home (**noun; object of the preposition**)
15. in (**preposition**) school (**noun; object of the preposition**)
16. of (**preposition**) iron (**noun; object of the preposition**)
17. of (**preposition**) stone (**noun; object of the preposition**)
18. with (**preposition**) the (**article**) exception (**noun**) of (**preposition**)
19. out (**preposition**) of (**preposition**)
20. in (**preposition**) front (**noun**) of (**preposition**)
21. against (**preposition**) my (**possessive pronoun adjective**) will (**noun; object of the preposition**)

IV.
Students were asked to underline at least one phrase and tell for which part of speech it stands in the sentence. The phrases are underlined and identified for you. Identifying the part of speech may be challenging for your student at this time, but wherever possible they should identify it. The coming chapters will explain in greater detail how to identify phrases.

1. The <u>Declaration of Independence</u> **(subject noun)** <u>was signed</u> **(verb phrase)** <u>in 1776</u>. **(adverbial phrase)**

2. The <u>House of Representatives</u> **(subject noun)** <u>has adjourned</u>. **(verb phrase)**

3. <u>Professor Edward Johnston</u> **(subject noun)** is now <u>in Sioux City</u>. **(adverbial phrase)**

4. The great <u>Desert of Sahara</u> **(subject noun)** is <u>in the Continent of Africa</u>. **(adverbial phrase; *Continent of Africa* is the object of the preposition)**

5. All were <u>on their feet</u> **(adverbial phrase)** <u>in a moment</u>. **(adverbial phrase)**

6. The preparations <u>for disembarking</u> **(adverbial phrase)** <u>had begun</u>. **(verb phrase)**

7. The <u>Pacific Mail Steamship Company</u> **(subject noun)** has an office <u>at this port</u>. **(adverbial phrase)**

8. Isabel shuddered <u>with horror</u>. **(adverbial phrase)**

9. I am a man <u>of peace</u>, **(adjective phrase)** though my abode now rings <u>with arms</u>. **(adverbial phrase)**

10. They <u>were</u> all <u>running</u> **(verb phrase)** <u>at full speed</u>. **(adverbial phrase)**

11. They <u>had fixed</u> **(verb phrase)** the wedding day.

12. There are many thousand Cinderellas <u>in London</u> **(adverbial phrase)**, and elsewhere <u>in England</u>. **(adverbial phrase)**

13. The maddened, terrified horse went <u>like the wind</u>. **(adverbial phrase)**

14. The <u>Prince of Wales</u> **(subject noun)** is heir <u>to the crown</u> **(adjective phrase)** <u>of England</u>. **(adjective phrase)**

15. "<u>In two days</u>," **(adverbial phrase)** Cromwell said coolly, "the city <u>will be</u> **(verb phrase)** <u>in our hands</u>." **(adverbial phrase)**

16. The scene <u>had</u> now <u>become</u> **(verb phrase)** <u>in the utmost degree</u> **(adverbial phrase)** animated and horrible.

17. There were upwards <u>of three hundred strangers</u> **(adverbial phrase)** <u>in the house</u>. **(adverbial phrase)**

18. The dog is not <u>of mountain breed</u>. **(predicate adjective)**

19. The boys <u>were coming</u> **(verb phrase)** <u>out of the grammar school</u> **(adverbial phrase)** <u>in shoals</u> **(adverbial phrase)**, laughing, running, whooping, as the manner <u>of boys</u> **(adjective phrase)** is.

20. My father walked <u>up and down the room</u> **(adverbial phrase)** <u>with impatience</u>. **(adverbial phrase)**

21. <u>Mr. Thomas Inkle</u> **(subject noun)** <u>of London</u> **(adjective phrase)**, aged twenty years, embarked <u>in the Downs</u> **(adverbial phrase)** <u>on the good ship</u> **(adverbial phrase)** called the Achilles, bound <u>for the West Indies</u>, **(adverbial phrase)** <u>on the 16th of June, 1647</u>, **(adverbial phrase)** in order to improve his fortune <u>by trade and merchandise</u>. **(adverbial phrase)**

Chapter 28: Adjective Phrases

I.

Students were instructed to place parentheses around the adjective phrases and draw an arrow to the substantive each describes or limits (bolded here).

1. A **man** (of strong understanding) is generally a **man** (of strong character). (*Thomas Carlyle (1795-1881)*, Robert Burns)

2. His flaxen **hair**, (of sunny hue),
   Curled closely round his bonnet blue.
   (*Sir Walter Scott (1771-1832)*, "Lady of the Lake")

3. Eastward was built a **gate** (of marble white). (*John Dryden (1631-1700)*, "Palamon and Arcite," a poem retelling the "A Knight's Tale")

4. He found a strong, fierce-looking **Highlander**, ((with an **axe**) (on his shoulder)), standing sentinel at the door. (*Sir Walter Scott (1771-1832)*, History of Scotland)

5. Hard by a **poplar** shook alway,
   All silver-green, (with gnarled bark).
   (*Alfred, Lord Tennyson (1809-1892)*, "Mariana")

6. The **gentleness** (of heaven) is on the sea. (*William Wordsworth (1770-1850)*, "By the Sea")

7. The **balustrade** (of the staircase) was also (of carved wood).

8. (Of stature fair), and slender frame,
   But firmly knit, was **Malcolm Graeme**.
   (*Sir Walter Scott (1771-1832)*, "Lady of the Lake")

9. It was a **lodge** (of ample size).

10. This gentleman was a **man** (of unquestioned courage).

11. An **emperor** (in his nightcap) would not meet with half the respect of an **emperor** (with a glittering crown). (*Oliver Goldsmith (1730-1774)*, Citizen of the World)

12. Our **affairs** are (in a bad condition).

13. Yathek arose in the morning with a **mind** (more at ease). (*William Beckford (1760-1844)*, The History of Caliph Vathek)

14. Her own mind was now in a **state** (of the utmost confusion).

15. Griffiths was a hard business **man**, (of shrewd, worldly good sense), but (of little refinement or cultivation). (*Washington Irving (1783-1859)*, Oliver Goldsmith)

II.

Students were instructed to substitute for each italicized adjective an adjective phrase without changing the general meaning of the sentence. Adjective phrases are shown in bolded italics, below.

1. The cashier was a man ***of strict honesty.***
2. A ravine ***of great depth*** checked our advance.
3. Brutus is a man ***of honor.***
4. Pillars ***of wood*** supported the roof.
5. The wanderer's clothing was ***of rags.***

6. The sailor carried a knife *with an ivory handle.*
7. The runner was quite *out of breath.*
8. The baron lived in the castle *of his ancestry.*
9. *Light of heart*, he rose in the morning.
10. Dr. Rush was a physician *of skill and experience.*

III.

Students were instructed to place parentheses around each adjective phrase and rewrite the sentence replacing the phrases with an adjective. Rewritten sentences are shown in bold, below.

1. Warrington was (of a quick and impetuous temper).
   Warrington was quick-tempered.

2. The road was not (of the most picturesque description).
   The road was not picturesque.

3. Fanny left the room (with a sorrowful heart).
   Heart-broken, Fanny left the room.
   (Jane Austen (1775-1817), Mansfield Park)

4. You are a man (of sense).
   You are a sensible man.

5. Upon the hero's head was a helmet (of brass).
   Upon the hero's head was a brass helmet.
   (Allusion to I Samuel 17:5)

6. Bring forth the goblets (of gold)!
   Bring forth gold goblets.

7. To scale the wall was a task (of great difficulty).
   To scale the wall was a difficult task.

8. The old soldier was (in poverty).
   The old soldier was impoverished.

9. We were all (in high spirits).
   We were all high-spirited.

10. A river (of great width) had to be crossed.
    A wide river had to be crossed.

11. He told his fellow-prisoners, in this darkest time, to be (of courage).
    He told his fellow-prisoners, in this darkest time, to be courageous.
    (John Dryden (1631-1700), "Heroes and Hero-Worship," about John Knox)

12. This is a matter (of importance).
    This is an important matter.

13. The beast glared at me (with eyes of fire).
    The beast glared at me with fiery eyes.

Chapter 28: Additional Exercises

I.

Students were instructed to analyze the sentences below. *Note: Students have not yet studied possessive or demonstrative pronouns (see #14 and 15 and Exercise II #4, 5 and 13). For now they may mark these as adjectives or leave them unlabeled. They are not asked to label adverbs or direct objects.*

1. The (Adj) **men** (S) (of Rome) (Adj) **hated** (V) kings.
2. A (Adj) **thing** (S) (of beauty) (Adj) **is** (V) a joy forever. *(John Keats (1795-1821), "A Thing of Beauty")*
3. **Steps** (S) (of marble) (Adj) **led** (V) up to the palace door.
4. A (Adj) **ladder** (S) (of ropes) (Adj) **hung** (V) from the balcony.
5. A (Adj) huge (Adj) **nugget** (S) (of gold) (Adj) **rewarded** (V) my search.
6. A (Adj) **book** (S) (with heavy clasps) (Adj) **was found** (V) in the chest.
7. The (Adj) **sword** (S) in his hand (Adj) **trembled** (V) violently.
8. A (Adj) **figure** (S) (with three angles) (Adj) **is** (V) a triangle.
9. The (Adj) **heights** (S) (above us) (Adj) **were shrouded** (V) in mist.
10. An (Adj) **animal** (S) (with four legs) (Adj) **is called** (V) a quadruped.
11. **Diamonds** (S) (from Africa) (Adj) **lay** (V) in the casket.
12. The (Adj) **subject** (S) (under discussion) (Adj) **was** fiercely **argued.** (V)
13. Rough (Adj) **herdsmen** (S) (from the mountains) (Adj) **filled** (V) the square.
14. My (Adj) **friends** (S) (at home) (Adj) **write** (V) to me seldom.
15. My (Adj) **uncle** (S) (in London) (Adj) **sent** (V) me an urgent message.
16. **Books** (S) (by the best authors) (Adj) **were** (V) his delight.
17. The (Adj) **silence** (S) (of the prairie) (Adj) **was** well-nigh terrible. *(Hamlin Garland (1860-1940),* Main-Traveled Roads)
18. The (Adj) **horse chestnuts** (S) (in the sheltered square) (Adj) **broke (V)** into blossom. *(Brander Matthews (1852-1929),* Vignettes of Manhattan) *Note: "Horse chestnuts" could be labeled as a subject phrase or "horse" could be labeled as the adjective of the subject "chestnuts." Accept either answer.*
19. A (Adj) **group** (S) (of strange children) (Adj) **ran** (V) at his heels. *(Washington Irving (1783-1859), "Rip Van Winkle")*
20. The (Adj) **light** (S) (on the mantel piece) (Adj) **had burnt** (V) low. *(Washington Irving (1783-1859),* Tales of a Traveler)
21. The (Adj) **customs** (S) (of mankind) (Adj) **are influenced** (V) by climate.
22. The (Adj) **tree** (S) (before his window) (Adj) **was** (V) a shabby sycamore. *(Brander Matthews (1852-1929),* Vignettes of Manhattan)
23. Before him **rose (V)** a (Adj) **gate** (S) (of marble white.) (Adj) *The subject and predicate are in reverse order here.*

II.

1. A (Adj) **giant** (S) (with three heads) (Adj) **lived** (V) in the cave.
2. A (Adj) **man** (S) (with a scythe) (Adj) **stood** (V) in the path.

3. <u>A (Adj)</u> **poodle** (S) <u>(with shaggy hair) (Adj)</u> **barked** (V) on the doorstep.
4. <u>That (Adj)</u> **castle** (S) <u>(on the cliff) (Adj)</u> **looks** (V) very ancient.
5. <u>His (Adj)</u> **money** (S) <u>(in the bank) (Adj)</u> **is** (V) his dearest possession.
6. <u>The (Adj)</u> **comrade** (S) <u>(by his side) (Adj)</u> **fell** (V) in the first attack.
7. <u>The (Adj)</u> **portraits** (S) <u>(on the wall) (Adj)</u> **frowned** (V) at him.
8. <u>The (Adj)</u> **bucket** (S) <u>(in the well) (Adj)</u> **was** (V) old and water-soaked.
9. <u>A (Adj)</u> big (Adj) **dog** (S) <u>(under the table) (Adj)</u> **growled** (V) and **showed** (V) his teeth.
10. <u>The (Adj)</u> **path** (S) <u>(by the brook) (Adj)</u> **wound** (V) pleasantly along.
11. <u>The (Adj)</u> **pain** (S) <u>(in his arm) (Adj)</u> **grew** (V) unendurable.
12. <u>The (Adj)</u> **road** (S) <u>(to ruin) (Adj)</u> **is** (V) all downhill.
13. <u>My (Adj)</u> **voyage** (S) <u>(among the islands) (Adj)</u> **lasted** (V) three days.
14. <u>The (Adj)</u> **smile** (S) <u>(on her lips) (Adj)</u> **faded.** (V)
15. <u>The (Adj)</u> **road** (S) <u>(through the forest) (Adj)</u> **is** (V) dangerous.
16. <u>The (Adj)</u> **man** (S) <u>(at the wheel) (Adj)</u> **was washed** (V) overboard.
17. <u>The (Adj)</u> **workmen** (S) <u>(in the factory) (Adj)</u> **struck** (V) for higher wages.

Chapter 29: Adverbial Phrases

I.

Students were instructed to use each of the adverbial phrases in Section 127, I and II, and those in Section 130 in a sentence. Check to see that they used the phrases properly. Answers will vary.

II.

Students were given a short list of adverbs with adverbial phrases which have the same meaning. They were instructed to write five more examples on the lines provided. Answers will vary.

Students were also instructed to write sentences using the examples and to read them aloud to you, substituting a phrase for the adverb.

III.

Students were instructed to place parentheses around the adverbial phrases and draw an arrow to what each modifies. The modified word is shown in bold print below.

1. Early (in the morning) a sudden storm **drove** us (within two or three leagues of Ireland). *(Daniel Defoe (1660-1731), Memoirs of a Cavalier)*

2. These things **terrified** the people (to the last degree). *(Daniel Defoe (1660-1731), A Journal of the Plague Year)*

3. ((At the first **glimpse**) of dawn) he **hastened** (to the prison). *(William Beckford (1760-1844), The History of Caliph Vathek) At the first glimpse modifies hastened, of dawn modifies glimpse.*

4. The wall **fell** (with a crash).

5. (By daybreak) we **had sailed** ((out of **sight**) of land). *Out of sight modifies had sailed; of land modifies sight.*

6. The full light of day **had** now **risen** (upon the desert). *(Thomas Moore (1779-1852), The Epicurean)*

7. (With smiles) the rising morn we **greet**. *(William Cowper (1731-1800), "The Fifth Satire of the First Book of Horace")*

8. Innumerable dismal stories we **heard** (every day). *(Daniel Defoe (1660-1731), History of the Plague in London)*

9. Homer **surpasses** all men (in this quality). *(Thomas Carlyle (1795-1881), "Essays")*

10. Her time **was filled** (by regular occupations). *(Edward Gibbon (1737-1794), Memoirs of My Life)*

11. I **say** this to you wholly (in confidence).

Chapter 30: Analysis: Phrases as Modifiers

I.

Students were instructed to analyze the sentences from chapter 29, Exercise III (reprinted below)

1. Early (**Adv**) (in the morning) (**Adv modifying** *drove*) a (**Adj**) sudden (**Adj**) <u>storm</u> | <u>drove</u> us [*Us* is the direct object, which students have not yet studied. It does not need to be labeled.] (within two or three leagues of Ireland) (**Adv**).

2. These (**Adj**) <u>things</u> | <u>terrified</u> the (**Adj**) people [direct object, does not need to be labeled] (to the last degree) (**Adv**).

3. ((At the first glimpse) (**Adv modifying** *hastened*) (of dawn) (**Adj modifying** *glimpse*)) <u>he</u> | <u>hastened</u> (to the prison) (**Adv**).

4. The (**Adj**) <u>wall</u> | <u>fell</u> (with a crash). (**Adv**)

5. (By daybreak) (**Adv modifying** *had sailed*) <u>we</u> | <u>had sailed</u> (out of sight) (**Adv modifying** *had sailed*)(of land). (**Adj modifying** *of land*)

6. The (**Adj**) full (**Adj**) <u>light</u> (of day) (**Adj**) | <u>had</u> now (**Adv**) <u>risen</u> (upon the desert). (**Adv**)

7. (With smiles) (**Adv**) the (**Adj**) rising (**Adj**) morn [direct object, does not need to be labeled] <u>we</u> | <u>greet</u>.

8. Innumerable (**Adj**) dismal (**Adj**) stories [direct object does not need to be labeled] <u>we</u> | <u>heard</u> (every day). (**Adv**)

9. <u>Homer</u> | <u>surpasses</u> all (**Adj**) men [direct object does not need to be labeled] (in this quality). (**Adv**)

10. Her (**Adj**) <u>time</u> | <u>was filled</u> (by regular occupations). (**Adv**) <u>I</u> | <u>say</u> this [direct object does not need to be labeled] (to you) (indirect object) wholly (**Adv**) (in confidence). (**Adv**)

II.

Students were instructed to place parentheses around all the prepositional phrases and label the adjective phrases with Adj or adverbial phrases with Adv. They were to draw an arrow to the noun or pronoun which the adjective phrase modifies, or to the verb, adjective, or adverb which the adverbial phrase modifies. (Shown in bold, below.)

1. A long journey **lay** (before us). (Adv)

2. The **kitchen** soon was all (on fire). (Adj)

3. The sea fowl **is gone** (to her nest); (Adv)
   The beast **is laid** down (in his lair). (Adv)
   (Attributed to Alexander Selkirk (1676-1721), known as the "real" Robinson Crusoe)

4. He was regarded as a **merchant** (of great wealth). (Adj)

5. The night was **Winter** (in his roughest mood). (Adj)
   (William Cowper (1731-1800), "A Winter Walk")

6. The chiming clocks (to dinner) (Adv) **call**.
   (Alexander Pope (1688-1744), Essay on Morals)

7. The **blanket** (of night) (Adj) is drawn **asunder** (for a moment). (Adv)
   (Thomas Carlyle (1795-1881), "Essays")

8. Green **pastures** she views ((in the **midst**) (Adj modifying *pastures*) (of the dale) (Adj modifying *midst*)).
   (William Wordsworth (1770-1850), "The Reverie of Poor Susan")

9. In this **state** (of breathless agitation) (Adj) **did** I **stand** (for some time). (Adv)
   (Thomas Moore (1779-1852), The Epicurean)

10. The **solution** (of this difficulty) (Adj) **must come** (from you). (Adv)
    (Jonathan Swift (1667-1745), Letters)

11. Grapevines here and there **twine** themselves (round shrub and tree). (Adv)   (Nathaniel Hawthorne (1804-1864), Mosses from an Old Manse)

12. Our coach **rattled** out (of the city). (Adv)
    (Nathaniel Hawthorne (1804-1864), "David Swan")

13. La Fleur **flew out** (of the room) (Adv modifying the adverb *out*) (like lightning) (Adv modifying *flew*).
    (Laurence Sterne (1713-1768), Sentimental Journey Through France and Italy)

14. Graham **came** ((from his hiding **place**) (Adv modifying *came*) (in the neighboring mountains) (Adj modifying *place*)).

15. Battles and skirmishes **were fought** (on all sides). (Adv)
    (Sir Walter Scott (1771-1832), Waverly Novels)

16. The stone **can**not **be moved** (from its place) (Adv) (by any force). (Adv)
    (Jonathan Swift (1667-1745), Gulliver's Travels)

17. (In silent horror) (Adv modifying *passed*) (o'er the boundless waste) (Adv modifying *passed*)
    The driver Hassan (with his camels) (Adv modifying *passed*) **passed**.
    (William Collins (1721-1759), "Hassan, or, The Camel-Driver")

18. They sat them **down** (upon the yellow sand), (Adv modifying the adverb *down*)
    (Between the sun and moon) (Adv modifying the adverb *down*)
    (upon the shore). (Adv modifying the adverb *down*)
    (Alfred, Lord Tennyson (1809-1892), "The Lotos-eaters)

19. Large towns **were founded** ((in different **parts**) (Adv) (of the kingdom) (Adj modifying *parts*)).

20. My days now **rolled** on ((in a perfect **dream**) (Adv modifying *rolled*) (of happiness) (Adj modifying *dream*)).
    (Thomas Moore (1779-1852), The Epicurean)

Chapter 30: Additional Exercises

Students were instructed to underline noun phrases once, verb and verb phrases twice, draw parentheses around adjective phrases and label with Adj, and draw square brackets around adverbial phrases and label with Adv.

1. The <u>British Parliament</u> and the <u>American Congress</u> <u>are</u> lawmaking bodies.

2. The <u>brave fireman</u> <u>had risked</u> his life.

3. We <u>were attacked</u> [on every side]. (Adv)

4. The <u>gates (of Amsterdam) (Adj phrase within the noun phrase)</u> <u>had been barred</u> against him. *(Thomas Macaulay (1800-1859),* History of England)

5. <u>Birds (of prey) (Adj phrase within the noun phrase)</u> <u>were wheeling</u> about.

6. I <u>have received</u> a letter (from my aunt).(Adj)

7. The <u>inn</u> <u>was beset</u> [by robbers]. (Adv) *(Washington Irving (1783-1859),* The Belated Travelers)

8. The <u>messenger</u> <u>was arrested</u> and <u>searched</u>, and the <u>letters</u> (from the enemy) (Adj) <u>were found</u>. *(Thomas Macaulay (1800-1859),* History of England)

9. The <u>roar (of guns)</u> (Adj phrase within the noun phrase) and the <u>clang (of bells)</u> (Adj phrase within the noun phrase) <u>lasted</u> [all night]. (Adv)

10. I <u>have come</u> here [without an invitation]. (Adv)

11. Tom <u>obeyed</u> [against his will]. (Adv)

12. [In spite of his efforts] (Adv) the <u>man</u> <u>could</u> not <u>swim</u> [against the tide]. (Adv)

13. A <u>huge alligator</u> <u>was sunning</u> himself [on the bank]. (Adv) *(Peter Hordern (c. 1878), "Among the Burmese")*

14. An <u>old dog</u> <u>cannot</u> <u>learn</u> new tricks. (no phrases)

15. <u>Speak</u> [in a loud, clear voice]. (Adv)

Chapter 31: Number

I.
Plural nouns are underlined and the singular form is given.

1. The stranger who would form a correct opinion of the English character must not confine his **observations** to the metropolis. He must go forth into the country; he must sojourn in **villages** and **hamlets**; he must visit **castles**, **villas**, **farmhouses**, **villages**; he must wander through **parks** and **gardens**, along **hedges** and green **lanes**; he must loiter about country **churches**; attend **wakes** and **fairs**, and other rural **festivals**; and cope with the people in all their **conditions** and all their **habits** and **humors**. *(Washington Irving (1783-1859), "Rural Life in England")*

   observation, village, hamlet, castle, villa, farmhouse, village, park, garden, hedge, lane, church, wake, fair, festival, condition, habit, humor

2. My raft was now strong enough to bear any reasonable weight. My next care was what to load it with, and how to preserve what I laid upon it from the surf of the sea. But I was not long considering this. I first laid all the plank or **boards** upon it that I could get; and, having considered well what I most wanted, I first got three of the seamen's **chests**, which I had broken open and emptied, and lowered them down upon my raft. The first of these I filled with **provisions**, — bread, rice, three Dutch **cheeses**, five **pieces** of dried goat's flesh, which we lived much upon, and a little remainder of European corn which had been laid by for some **fowls** which we brought to sea with us; but the **fowls** were killed. There had been some barley and wheat together, but, to my great disappointment, I found afterwards that the rats had eaten or spoiled it all. *(Daniel Defoe (1660-1731), Robinson Crusoe)*

   board, chest, provision, cheese, piece, fowl, fowl

3. **Weavers**, **nailers**, **rope makers**, **artisans** of every degree and calling, thronged forward to join the procession from every gloomy and narrow street. *(Sir Walter Scott (1771-1832), Quentin Durward)*

   weaver, nailer, rope maker, artisan

II.
Students were instructed to write a description of some farm, or piece of woods, or town, or village, that they know well. Check their paragraph and check that they labeled nouns N and adjectives Adj. They were also instructed to give the plural of every noun that they have used in the singular and the singular of every plural noun.

Chapter 32: Genitive or Possessive Case

Each blank is filled with a genitive (possessive modifier). Answers will vary. Suggestions are given below.

1. The __man's__ efforts were successful.
2. The _soldier's_ life was spared at the request of his comrades.
3. _John's_ brother lives in Kentucky.
4. The _raccoon's_ paw was caught in the trap.
5. The __boy's__ rifle went off by accident.
6. The _captain's_ bravery saved the ship with all the passengers.
7. The __girl's__ eyes shone with excitement.

Chapter 33: Forms of the Genitive

I.

Students were instructed to underline all the genitives (possessive modifiers) and draw an arrow to the noun or pronoun that it modifies (shown in bold below).

1. The <u>emperor's</u> **palace** is in the center of the city, where the two great streets meet. *(Jonathan Swift (1667-1745),* Gulliver's Travels*)*

2. <u>Oliver's</u> **education** began when he was about three years old. *(Washington Irving (1783-1859),* Oliver Goldsmith*)*

3. Caesar scorns the <u>poet's</u> **lays.** *(Alexander Pope (1688-1744), "Satire")*

4. The silver light, with quivering glance,
    Played on the <u>water's</u> still **expanse.**
    (Sir Walter Scott (1771-1832), "Lady of the Lake")

5. Here on this beach a hundred years ago,
    Three children of three houses, Annie Lee,
    The prettiest little damsel in the port,
    And Philip Ray, the <u>miller's</u> only **son,**
    And Enoch Arden, a rough <u>sailor's</u> **lad,**
    Made orphan by a winter shipwreck, played
    Among the waste and lumber of the shore.
    (Alfred, Lord Tennyson (1809-1892), "Enoch Arden")

6. It is not the greatness of a <u>man's</u> **means** that makes him independent, so much as the smallness of his wants.
    (William Cobbett (1763-1835))

7. In faith and hope the world will disagree,
    But all <u>mankind's</u> **concern** is charity.
    (Alexander Pope (1688-1744), "Essay on Man")

8. The <u>jester's</u> **speech** made the duke laugh. *(Sir Walter Scott (1771-1832),* Quentin Durward*)*

9. A <u>man's</u> **nature** runs either to herbs or weeds. *(Francis Bacon (1561-1626), "Essays, Civil and Moral")*

II.

Students were instructed to write sentences containing the genitive singular of each of the following nouns. Sentences will vary. Genitive singular of each word is given below.

1. boy	boy's	12. captain	captain's
2. girl	girl's	13. sailor	sailor's
3. dog	dog's	14. soldier	soldier's
4. cat	cat's	15. chieftain	chieftain's
5. John	John's	16. Shakespeare	Shakespeare's
6. Mary	Mary's	17. Milton	Milton's
7. Sarah	Sarah's	18. Whittier	Whittier's
8. William	William's	19. baker	baker's
9. spider	spider's	20. manufacturer	manufacturer's
10. frog	frog's	21. chimney sweep	chimney sweep's
11. elephant	elephant's		

III.

Students were instructed to write sentences containing the genitive of the names of twelve persons whom you know. Answers will vary.

IV.

Genitives are underlined and marked (S) singular or (P) plural.

1. The **monarch's (S)** wrath began to rise. *(Lord Byron (1788-1824), "Siege and Conquest of Alhama")*

2. They err who imagine that this **man's (S)** courage was ferocity. *(Thomas Carlyle (1795-1881),* Spiritual Portrait of Luther*)*

3. Two **years' (P)** travel in distant and barbarous countries has accustomed me to bear privations. *(Lord Byron (1788-1824), "Byron's Reflections on Himself")*

4. Hark! hark! the lark at **heaven's (S)** gate sings. *(William Shakespeare (1564-1616),* Cymbeline*)*

5. Portia dressed herself and her maid in **men's (P)** apparel. *(Charles and Mary Lamb's* Tales from Shakespeare, *"Merchant of Venice")*

6. He waved his **huntsman's (S)** cap on high. *(Sir Walter Scott (1771-1832), "The Wild Hunter")*

7. The **Porters' (P)** visit was all but over. *(Thomas Hughes (1822-1896),* Tom Brown at Oxford*)*

8. The **ladies' (P)** colds kept them at home all the evening.

9. The crags repeat the **ravens' (P)** croak. *(William Wordsworth (1770-1850), "Fidelity")*

10. **Farmer Grove's (S)** house is on fire!

11. The Major paced the terrace in front of the house for his two **hours' (P)** constitutional walk. *(William Makepeace Thackeray (1811-1863),* History of Pendennis*)*

V.

Students were instructed to write sentences containing the genitive plural of all the common nouns in Exercise II. Answers will vary. Genitive plural of each noun is given below.

1.	boy	boys'	12.	captain	captains'
2.	girl	girls'	13.	sailor	sailors'
3.	dog	dogs'	14.	soldier	soldiers'
4.	cat	cats'	15.	chieftain	chieftains'
5.	John	N/A	16.	Shakespeare	N/A
6.	Mary	N/A	17.	Milton	N/A
7.	Sarah	N/A	18.	Whittier	N/A
8.	William	N/A	19.	baker	bakers'
9.	spider	spiders'	20.	manufacturer	manufacturers'
10.	frog	frogs'	21.	chimney sweep	chimney sweeps'
11.	elephant	elephants'			

VI.

Insert the apostrophe in the proper place in every word that needs it.

1. The **man's** hair was black.
2. The **men's** courage was almost gone.
3. The **spider's** web was too weak to hold the flies.

4. The whole clan bewailed the **warrior's** death.
5. The **soldiers'** helmets were visible.
6. I gave him a **month's** notice.
7. Six **months'** time had elapsed.
8. **Women's** wages are lower than **men's**.
9. A **woman's** wit has saved many a stupid man.
10. The **chieftain's** sons are the most devoted of brothers.

Chapter 34: Genitive of Pronouns (Possessive Pronouns)

Answers will vary. Make sure that students have made proper sentences for each pronoun.

Chapter 35: Genitive Replaced by an *Of*-Phrase

I.
Be sure that students have written twenty sentences properly, then check that the twenty additional sentences have properly used the *of*-phrase. Answers will vary.

II.
Check that your student's sentences properly use the genitive form of the words given. Answers will vary.

Chapter 36: Analysis: Genitive and *Of*-Phrase

Students were instructed to analyze the sentences below.

1. The (**Adj**) chieftain's (**Adj**) <u>brow</u> | <u>darkened</u>. *(John Buchan (1875-1940)*, Huntingtower)
2. Quickly (**Adv**) <u>sped</u> | the (**Adj**) <u>hours</u> (of that happy day). (**Adj**)
3. Their (**Adj**) <u>friends</u> | <u>have abandoned</u> them. (Direct object, does not need to be labeled)
4. Edison's (**Adj**) great (**Adj**) <u>discovery</u> | <u>was</u> then (**Adv**) <u>announced</u>.
5. The (**Adj**) <u>population</u> (of Chicago) (**Adj**) | <u>is increasing</u> rapidly. (**Adv**)
6. The (**Adj**) <u>captain</u> (of the steamer) (**Adj**) | <u>stood</u> (on the bridge). (**Adv**)
7. The (**Adj**) men's (**Adj**) last (**Adj**) <u>hope</u> | <u>had vanished</u>.
8. Our (**Adj**) <u>distress</u> | <u>was</u> soon (**Adv**) <u>relieved</u>.
9. The (**Adj**) <u>branches</u> (of the tree) (**Adj**) | <u>droop</u> gracefully. (**Adv**)
10. The (**Adj**) bird's (**Adj**) <u>song</u> | <u>rang</u> out (**Adv**) merrily. (**Adv**)
11. A (**Adj**) huntsman's (**Adj**) <u>life</u> | <u>had</u> always (**Adv**) <u>attracted</u> me. (**Direct object, does not need to be labeled**)

Chapter 37: Apposition

I.

Students were instructed to fill the blanks with appositives. Answers will vary. Suggestions are given.

1. Mr. Jones, the __contractor__ , is building a house for me.
2. Have you seen Rover, my __dog__ , anywhere?
3. Animals of all kinds, __monkeys__ , __lions__ , __tigers__ , and __hippos__ , were exhibited in the menagerie.
4. Chapman, the __captain__ of the team, broke his collar bone.
5. My new kite, __a gift__ from my uncle, is caught in the tree.
6. Washington, the __President__ of the United States, is on the Potomac.
7. Who has met my young friend __Jack__ today? *Note: See Appendix F - Commas #7, Note 2 in text.*
8. Charles I, __King__ of England, was beheaded in 1649.
9. Washington, the __President__ of his country, was born in 1732.
10. Tiger-hunting, a dangerous __pursuit__ , was the sultan's chief delight.

II.

Students were instructed to underline the appositives, and circle the noun (bolded below) to which each is attached.

1. An **Englishwoman**, <u>the wife of one of the officers</u>, was sitting on the battlements with her child in her arms. *(Sir Walter Scott (1771-1832), History of Scotland)*

2. I went to visit **Mr. Hobbes**, <u>the famous philosopher</u>. *(Samuel Pepys (1633-1703), Diary)*

3. We were hopeful **boys**, <u>all three of us</u>. *(Daniel Defoe (1660-1731), The Life of Colonel Jack)*

4. **Spring**, <u>the sweet Spring</u>, is the year's pleasant king. *(Thomas Nash (1567-1601), "Spring")*

5. Then forth they all out of their baskets drew
   Great store of **flowers**, <u>the honor of the field</u>.
   (Edmund Spenser (1552-1599), "Prothalamion")

6. He was speedily summoned to the apartment of his **captain**, <u>the Lord Crawford</u>. *(Sir Walter Scott (1771-1832), Quentin Durward)*

7. No rude **sound** shall reach thine ear,
   <u>Armor's clang and war-steed champing</u>.
   (Sir Walter Scott (1771-1832), "Song")

8. And thus spake on that ancient **man**,
   <u>The bright-eyed mariner</u>.
   (Samuel Taylor Coleridge (1722-1834), "The Rime of the Ancient Mariner")

9. There lived at no great distance from this stronghold a **farmer**, <u>a bold and stout man</u>, whose name was Binnock. *(Sir Walter Scott (1771-1832), History of Scotland)*

Chapter 38: Analysis: The Appositive

I.

Students were instructed to underline the appositives.

1. Stuart, <u>the dauntless explorer</u>, perished in the desert.
2. Spring, <u>the sweet spring</u>, is the year's pleasant king. *(Thomas Nashe (1567-1601), "Spring, the Sweet Spring")*
3. Quentin's captain, <u>the Lord Crawford</u>, summoned him. *(Sir Walter Scott (1771-1832), adapted from* Quentin Durward)
4. The hiss of the serpent, <u>a blood-curdling sound</u>, was heard in the darkness.
5. The old sailor, <u>a weather-beaten Scot</u>, told a strange story.
6. The farmer, <u>a bold, strong man</u>, lived not far from the fort.
7. We, <u>your oldest friends</u>, will help you.
8. The castle, <u>a battered ruin</u>, stood by the river.
9. Ferguson, <u>an earnest patriot</u>, addressed the crowd.

II.

Students were instructed to analyze the sentences in Exercise I, reproduced below, according to the steps given.

1. **Stuart (S)**, the (**Adj**) dauntless (**Adj**) explorer (**A**), **perished (V) in the desert**.
2. **Spring (S)**, the (**Adj**) sweet (**Adj**) spring (**A**), **is (V) the year's pleasant king**. *(Thomas Nashe (1567-1601), "Spring, the Sweet Spring")*
3. Quentin's **captain (S)**, the (**Adj**) Lord Crawford (**A**), **summoned (V)** him. *(Sir Walter Scott (1771-1832), adapted from* Quentin Durward)
4. The **hiss (S)** of the serpent, a (**Adj**) blood-curdling (**Adj**) sound (**A**), **was heard (V) in the darkness**.
5. The old **sailor (S)**, a (**Adj**) weather-beaten (**Adj**) Scot (**A**), **told (V) a strange story**.
6. The **farmer (S)**, a (**Adj**) bold (**Adj**), strong (**Adj**) man (**A**), **lived (V) not far from the fort**.
7. **We (S)**, your (**Adj**) oldest (**Adj**) friends (**A**), **will help (V) you**.
8. The **castle (S)**, a (**Adj**) battered (**Adj**) ruin (**A**), **stood (V) by the river**.
9. **Ferguson (S)**, an (**Adj**) earnest (**Adj**) patriot (**A**), **addressed (V) the crowd**.

Chapter 39: Transitive and Intransitive Verbs — The Direct Object

I.
Verbs and verb phrases are underlined and labels T (transitive) or I (intransitive). Direct objects are labeled with DO.

1. A small party of the musketeers **followed (T)** me **(DO)**. *(Daniel Defoe (1660-1731),* Memoirs of a Cavalier*)*

2. **These (DO)**, therefore, I **can pity (T)**. *(William Cowper (1731-1800),* The Task*)*

3. Through the darkness and the cold we **flew (I)**. *(William Wordsworth (1770-1850), "The Prelude")*

4. Yet I **insisted (I)**, yet you **answered (I)** not. *(William Shakespeare (1564-1616),* Julius Caesar*)*

5. The enemy **made (T)** frequent and desperate **sallies (DO)**. *(Daniel Defoe (1660-1731),* Memoirs of a Cavalier*)*

6. Fierce passions **discompose (T)** the **mind (DO)**. *(William Cowper (1731-1800), "Contentment")*

7. The gallant greyhounds swiftly **ran (I)**. *(Author unknown,* The Ballad of Chevy Chase*)*

8. The Scots **killed (T)** the **cattle (DO)** of the English.

9. Down the ashes **shower (I)** like rain. *(Lord Byron (1788-1824), "The Siege of Corinth")*

10. While Spain **built (T)** up her **empire (DO)** in the New World, the English seamen **reaped (T)** a humbler **harvest (DO)** in the fisheries of New-Foundland. *(John Richard Green (1837-1883),* History of the English People*)*

II.
Students were instructed to fill in the blanks with pronouns in the objective case. Answers will vary. Suggestions are given.

1. They found __**him**__ in the woods.
2. My friend asked __**me**__ to dinner.
3. The savage dog bit __**her**__ severely.
4. Our teacher has sent __**us**__ home.
5. Their uncle visited __**them**__ last week.
6. The rain drenched __**me**__ in spite of my umbrella.
7. Mary's brother helped__**her**__ with her lesson.
8. Arthur's book interests __**him**__ very much.
9. The flood drove __**us**__ from our farm.
10. A boat carried __**us**__ across the river.

Chapter 40: Analysis: The Direct Object

I.
Students were instructed to analyze the following sentences.

1. **D**   Jane **(S)**   wrote **(V-T)** a **(Adj)** hurried **(Adj)** note **(DO)**.

2. **D**   The **(Adj)** baron **(S)**   pardoned **(V-T)** the **(Adj)** young **(Adj)** couple **(DO)**.
    (Washington Irving (1783-1859), "The Specter Bridegroom")

3. **D**   Every **(Adj)** science **(S)**   has **(V)** its **(Adj)** undiscovered **(Adj)** mysteries **(DO)**.

4. **D**   We **(S)**   heard **(V-T)** the **(Adj)** sound **(DO)** (of music) **(Adj)** (in the distance) **(Adv)**.
    (Washington Irving (1783-1859), "The Sketch Book")

5. **D**   He **(S)**   turned **(V-I)** away **(Adv)** and strode **(V)** off **(Adv)** (in the opposite direction) **(Adv)**.
    (Edith Wharton (1862-1937), The Fruit of the Tree)

6. **D**   The **(Adj)** sheep **(S)** and the **(Adj)** cow **(S)**   have **(V)** no **(Adv)** cutting **(Adj)** teeth **(DO)**
    (in the upper jaw) **(Adj)**.

7. **D**   A **(Adj)** tap **(S)** (on her door) **(Adj)**   interrupted **(V-T)** these **(Adj)** musings **(DO)**.
    (Edith Wharton (1862-1937), The Fruit of the Tree)

8. **D**   Bessy's **(Adj)** lip **(S)**   trembled **(V)** (and) the **(Adj)** color **(S)**   sprang **(V)** (to her face) **(Adv)**.

9. **D, E**   How **(Adv)** had **(V)**   the **(Adj)** gentle **(Adj)** spirit **(S)** (of that good man) **(Adj)** sweetened **(V-T)**
    our **(Adj)** natures! **(DO)**
    (Washington Irving (1783-1859), Tales of a Traveler)

II.
Analyze the following sentences as you did in Exercise I.

1. **D, E**   How **(Adv)** I **(S)**   envied **(V-T)** the **(Adj)** happy **(Adj)** groups **(DO)** (on the tops) **(Adj)**
    (of the stagecoaches) **(Adj)**!
    (Washington Irving (1783-1859), Tales of a Traveler)

2. **D**   The **(Adj)** carriage **(S)**   came **(V)** on **(Adv)** (at a furious rate) **(Adv)**.
    (Washington Irving (1783-1859), adapted from Tales of a Traveler)

3. **D**   The **(Adj)** Highlanders **(S)**   suddenly **(Adv)** flung **(V-T)** away **(Adv)** their **(Adj)**
    muskets **(DO)**, drew **(V-T)** their **(Adj)** broadswords **(DO)**, and rushed **(V)** forward **(Adv)** (with a
    fearful yell) **(Adv)**. *Note: Be sure students have noticed the compound verbs (transitive and intransitive) that
    go with the subject Highlanders.*
    (Thomas Macaulay (1800-1859), History of England)

4. **D**   I **(S)**   see **(V-T)** the **(Adj)** path **(DO)** (of duty) **(Adj)** (before me) **(Adj)**.

5. **D**   Nothing **(S)**   could resist **(V-T)** their **(Adj)** onset **(DO)**.

6. **D**   The **(Adj)** fleet **(S)**   bombarded **(V-T)** the **(Adj)** town **(DO)**.

7. **D** A (**Adj**) crowd (**S**) (of children) (**Adj**) was following (**V-T**) the (**Adj**) piper (**DO**) (about the streets) (**Adv**).

8. **D** Streams (**S**) (of lava) (**Adj**) rolled (**V**) (down the side) (**Adv**) (of the mountain) (**Adj**).
   Note: "Rolled" in this instance is an intransitive verb, not transitive.

9. **D** The (**Adj**) anchor (**S**) would (**V**) not (**Adv**) hold (**V-T**) the (**Adj**) ship (**DO**).

10. **D** The (**Adj**) bomb (**S**) exploded (**V**) and scattered (**V-T**) destruction (**DO**).

11. **D** The (**Adj**) tide (**S**) ebbed (**V**) and left (**V-T**) the (**Adj**) boat (**DO**) (on the bar) (**Adv**).

12. **D** A (**Adj**) terrible (**Adj**) earthquake (**S**) has (**V**) almost (**Adv**) destroyed (**V-T**) the (**Adj**) city (**DO**).

13. **D** The (**Adj**) flames (**S**) poured (**V**) out (**Adv**) (of the upper windows) (**Adv**) (of the factory) (**Adj**).

14. **D** The (**Adj**) conspirators (**S**) attacked (**V-T**) Caesar (**DO**) (in the Senate-house) (**Adv**).
   He (**S**) resisted (**V-T**) them (**DO**) (for a time) (**Adv**), but (at last) (**Adv**) fell (**V**) (at the foot) (**Adv**) (of Pompey's statue) (**Adj**).

Chapter 41: Active and Passive Voice

I.
Students were instructed to underline the passive verbs and verb phrases and label the subject of each sentence with an S. The subject is shown in bold here.

1. My **command** <u>was</u> promptly <u>obeyed</u>.

2. **One** of the men who robbed me <u>was taken</u>.

3. Now <u>were</u> the **gates** of the city <u>broken</u> down by General Monk. *(John Evelyn (1620-1706), "The Diary of John Evelyn")*

4. Suddenly, while I gazed, the loud **crash** of a thousand cymbals <u>was heard</u>. *(Thomas Moore (1779-1852), The Epicurean)*

5. **Judgment** <u>is forced</u> upon us by experience. *(Samuel Johnson (1709-1784), "The Lives of English Poets")*

6. **Nature** <u>is</u> often <u>hidden</u>, sometimes <u>overcome</u>, seldom <u>extinguished</u>. *(Francis Bacon (1561-1626), "Of Nature of Men")*

7. **Youth** <u>is</u> always <u>delighted</u> with applause. *(Samuel Johnson (1709-1784), The History of Rasselas, Prince of Abyssinia: A Tale)*

8. The **hall** <u>was</u> immediately <u>cleared</u> by the soldiery.

9. Just before midnight the **castle** <u>was blown</u> up.

10. My **spirits** <u>were raised</u> by the rapid motion of the journey. *(Edward Gibbon (1737-1794), Memoirs of My Life)*

11. A great **council** of war <u>was held</u> in the king's quarters. *(Daniel Defoe (1660-1731), Memoirs of a Cavalier)*

12. Many **consciences** <u>were awakened</u>; many hard **hearts** <u>were melted</u> into tears; many a penitent **confession** <u>was made</u>. *(Daniel Defoe (1660-1731), A Journal of the Plague Year)*

II.
Students were instructed to change the active voice to the passive voice. Passive voice sentences are shown in bold on the right.

1. The sailor rescued the child.	**The child was rescued by the sailor.**
2. Columbus discovered America.	**America was discovered by Columbus.**
3. The French settled Louisiana.	**Louisiana was settled by the French.**
4. Intemperance wrecked the man's life.	**The man's life was wrecked by intemperance.**
5. Edward VII succeeded Victoria.	**Victoria was succeeded by Edward VII.**
6. The Americans captured Major André.	**Major André was captured by the Americans.**
7. Longfellow wrote "Hiawatha."	**"Hiawatha" was written by Longfellow.**
8. Robert Fulton invented the steamboat.	**The steamboat was invented by Robert Fulton.**
9. Exercises in analysis sharpen our wits.	**Our wits are sharpened by exercises in analysis.**
10. An eclipse of the sun terrified the savages.	**The savages were terrified by an eclipse of the sun.**
11. Julius Caesar twice invaded Britain.	**Britain was invaded twice by Julius Caesar.**
12. Tom's clever play won the game.	**The game was won by Tom's clever play.**
13. A landslide buried the house.	**The house was buried by a landslide.**
14. Lightning struck the statue.	**The statue was struck by lightning.**
15. Her brother's unkindness grieved Jane.	**Jane was grieved by her brother's unkindness.**

Chapter 42: Predicate Adjective

Students were instructed to circle the predicate adjectives (shown in bold here) and underline the subject of the sentence which is described by the predicate adjective.

1. The <u>river</u> was now **full** of life and motion. *(Thomas Moore (1779-1852), The Epicurean)*
2. The <u>sentiments</u> of the hearers were **various**. *(Samuel Johnson (1709-1784), The History of Rasselas, Prince of Abyssinia: A Tale)*
3. In the north the <u>storm</u> grew **thick**. *(Daniel Defoe (1660-1731), Memoirs of a Cavalier)*
4. Soon his <u>eyes</u> grew **brilliant**. *(John Keats (1795-1821), "The Eve of St. Agnes")*
5. Some <u>fortifications</u> still remained **entire**. *(Fanny Burney (1752-1840), Cecilia: Or Memoirs of an Heiress)*
6. <u>He</u> lay **prostrate** on the ground.
7. The <u>evening</u> proved **fine**.
8. <u>Alfred Burnham</u> has become **penitent**. *(William Black (1841-1898), Kilmeny)*
9. How **different** the <u>place</u> looked now!
10. <u>She</u> seemed **anxious** to get away without speaking.
11. Their <u>hearts</u> are grown **desperate**. *(John Bunyan (1628-1688), The Pilgrim's Progress)*
12. The <u>captain</u> appeared **impatient**.
13. <u>He</u> began to look a little less **stern** and **terrible**. *(Daniel Defoe (1660-1731), The Life of Colonel Jack)*
14. Many <u>houses</u> were then left **desolate**. *(Daniel Defoe (1660-1731), A Journal of the Plague Year)*
15. <u>Gertrude</u> remained **aghast** and **motionless**. *(Susan Ferrier (1782-1854), The Inheritance)*
16. <u>He</u> stood **stubborn** and **rigid**. *(Charlotte Brontë (1816-1855), Jane Eyre)*
17. All my <u>efforts</u> were **(in vain)**.
18. These <u>threats</u> sounded **alarming**.
19. The same <u>law</u> holds **good**.
20. <u>She</u> seemed **anxious** and looked **pale**.
21. Such <u>conduct</u> is thought **improper**.
22. The <u>air</u> was **fresh** but **balmy**.
23. <u>He</u> lay for a long while **motionless** and **silent**. *(Brander Matthews (1852-1929), Vignettes of Manhattan)*
24. A great <u>part</u> of the island is rather **level**. *(Washington Irving (1783-1859), "Legend of Sleepy Hollow")*
25. Their <u>conversation</u> was **gay** and **animated**.
26. <u>He</u> had become **sluggish** and **self-indulgent**. *(Thomas Macaulay (1800-1859), History of England)*
27. <u>Martha</u> was **blunt** and **plain-spoken** to a fault. *(Elizabeth Gaskell (1810-1865), Cranford)*
28. In the tall towers by the wayside the <u>bells</u> hung **mute**. *(Augustus Jessopp (1823-1914), The Black Death in East Anglia)*
29. <u>Lochiel</u> was **wise** in council, **eloquent** in debate, **ready** in devising expedients, and **skillful** in managing the minds of men. *(Thomas Macaulay (1800-1859), History of England)*
30. <u>Captain Brown and Miss Jenkyns</u> were not very **cordial** to each other. *(Elizabeth Gaskell (1810-1865), Cranford)*

II.

Students were instructed to fill in each blank with a **predicate adjective**. Answers will vary. Suggestions are given.

1. The storm came on very suddenly. The whole landscape became __**soaked**__.
2. The lake is __**swollen**__ today.
3. Seals look __**fierce**__, but are not dangerous.
4. The dog proved __**obedient**__ to his master.
5. Washington was __**first**__ in war and __**first**__ in peace.
6. The leaves turn __**golden**__ in the autumn.
7. John has grown very __**tall**__ in the past year.
8. Every lesson seems __**long**__ to the indolent.
9. Such conduct appears __**improper**__ to me.
10. Do not look so __**downcast**__.
11. Why does Mary seem so __**unhappy**__?
12. Is the ice __**frozen**__? It looks __**solid**__ enough.
13. You do not appear very __**tired**__.
14. The iron grew __**hot**__ in the fire.
15. Your affection for you friend has grown __**cold**__.
16. The weather has been __**chilly**__ of late.
17. Be __**patient**__, and you will be __**content**__.
18. Never be __**careless**__, for carelessness is stupidity.

Chapter 43: Predicate Nominative

I.

Students were instructed to make seven sentences containing a predicate nominative after *am, is, are, was, were, has been, or had been*. They were to use subjects from the list provided. Suggestions are given.

1. am: **"I, Thomas Jefferson, am a Founding Father."** (Obviously, the verb *am* cannot be used with a subject other than *I*. Here we offer a sentence with an appositive. If you student is stymied, encourage them that they do not need to use a subject from the list for *am*.)
2. is: **The story is an epic tale.**
3. are: **Oranges are a citrus fruit.**
4. was: **The war was a misery.**
5. were: **The scissors were a sharp tool.**
6. has been: **Peace has been a gift.**
7. had been: **Carlo had been a student.**

II.

Answers will vary, but the student's predicate nominative should be a noun and should make sense.

1. Thomas Smith is my ___**friend**___ .
2. My father's name is **John** .
3. A noun is the ___**name**___ of a person, place, or thing.
4. A pronoun is a ___**word**___ used instead of a noun.
5. The banana is a delicious ___**fruit**___ .
6. The boys are all ___**students**___ .
7. Napoleon was ___**emperor**___ of France.
8. Albert has been your ___**friend**___ for many years.
9. We had been ___**tourists**___ in England.
10. My birthday present will be a ___**bicycle**___ .
11. Fire is a good ___**servant**___ but a bad ___**master**___ .
12. Hunger is the best ___**sauce**___ .
13. Our five senses are ___**sight**___ , ___**hearing**___ , ___**taste**___ , ___**touch**___ , and ___**smell**___ .
14. My favorite flower has always been the ___**daisy**___ .
15. A friend in need is a ___**friend**___ indeed.
16. Virtue is its own ___**reward**___ .
17. My favorite game is ___**chess**___ .
18. Milton was an English ___**poet**___ .
19. "Hiawatha" is a ___**poem**___ by Longfellow.
20. Benjamin Franklin was a ___**printer**___ .
21. John Adams was the second ___**President**___ of the United States.

Chapter 44: Direct Object and Predicate Nominative Distinguished

I.
Students were instructed to underline the subjects once, the simple predicates twice, and to label the predicate nominative PN (shown in bold print here).

1. He is an honest **man** and an honest **writer**.

2. The Malay has been a fearful **enemy** for months. (*Thomas De Quincey (1785-1859)*, Confessions of an English Opium-Eater)

3. King Malcolm was a brave and wise **prince**. (*Sir Walter Scott (1771-1832)*, History of Scotland)

4. You had been the great **instrument** of preserving your country from foreign and domestic ruin. (*Jonathan Swift (1667-1745)*, "Letter to Lord-Treasurer Oxford")

5. Still he continued an incorrigible **rascal**.

6. Dewdrops are the **gems** of morning,
   But the **tears** of mournful eve.
   (*Samuel Taylor Coleridge (1722-1834)*, "Youth and Age")

7. While still very young, she became the **wife** of a Greek adventurer. (*Thomas Moore (1779-1852)*, The Epicurean)

8. Every instant now seemed an **age**.

9. Dr. Daniel Dove was a perfect **doctor**, and his horse Nobs was a perfect **horse**. (*Robert Southey (1774-1843)*, The Doctor)

10. Francis the First stood before my mind the **abstract** and **model** of perfection and greatness. (*William Godwin (1756-1836)*, Travels of St. Leon)

11. The name of Francis Drake became the **terror** of the Spanish Indies. (*John Richard Green (1837-1883)*, History of the English People)

12. Great barkers are no **biters**.

13. I hope [she will prove a well-disposed **girl**]. *Note: In this sentence the clause, shown in brackets, functions as the direct object of "hope."* (*Jane Austen (1775-1817)*, Mansfield Park)

14. He may prove a troublesome **appendage** to us. (*Susan Ferrier (1782-1854)*, The Inheritance)

15. His bridge was only loose **planks** laid upon large trestles. (*Daniel Defoe (1660-1731)*, Memoirs of a Cavalier)

16. I entered the town a **candle-snuffer**, and I quitted it a **hero**! (*Oliver Goldsmith (1730-1774)*, "Essays")

17. A very complaisant and agreeable companion may, and often does, prove a very improper and a very dangerous **friend**. *Note: In this sentence a compound verb phrase links "companion" to the predicate nominative "friend."* (*Philip Dormer Stanhope, Earl of Chesterfield (1694-1773)*, "Lord Chesterfield's Letters")

18. Real friendship is a slow **grower**. (*Philip Dormer Stanhope, Earl of Chesterfield (1694-1773)*, "Lord Chesterfield's Letters")

19. He became a **friend** of Mrs. Wilberforce's.

20. My friends fall around me, and I shall be left a lonely **tree** before I am withered. *Note: Only the clause containing "I shall be" has a predicate nominative. Students should identify all the subjects and verbs.* (*Lord Byron (1788-1824)*, Letters and Journals of Lord Byron)

II.

Students were instructed to label the predicate nominatives with PN and the direct objects with DO. They are bolded and labeled below.

1. With how sad steps, O Moon, thou climb'st the **sky (DO)**! *(Sir Philip Sidney (1554-1586), "Astrophel and Stella")*

2. The landscape was a **forest (PN)** wide and bare. *(John Dryden (1631-1700), "Palamon and Arcite," a poem retelling the "A Knight's Tale")*

3. Here the Albanian proudly treads the **ground (DO)**. *(Lord Byron (1788-1824), "Childe Harold's Pilgrimage")*

4. Wing thy **flight (DO)** from hence on the morrow. *Note: The subject of this imperative sentence is implied "you." (Sir Walter Scott (1771-1832), Woodstock)*

5. It was a wild and strange **retreat (PN)**
    As e'er was trod by outlaw's feet.
    (Sir Walter Scott (1771-1832), "Lady of the Lake")

6. Honor is the **subject (PN)** of my story. *(William Shakespeare (1564-1616), Julius Caesar)*

7. I alone became their **prisoner (PN)**. *(William Shakespeare (1564-1616), Hamlet)*

8. A strange **group (PN)** we were.

9. The mountain mist took **form (DO)** and **limb (DO)**
    Of noontide hag or goblin grim.
    (Sir Walter Scott (1771-1832), "Lady of the Lake")

10. The family specialties were **health**, **good-humor**, and **vivacity. (PNs)** *(Henry Kingsley (1830-1876), The Hillyars and the Burtons: A Story of Two Families)*

11. The deep war-drum's sound announced the **close (DO)** of day. *(Lord Byron (1788-1824), "Childe Harold's Pilgrimage")*

12. You seem a sober ancient **gentleman (PN)**. *(William Shakespeare (1564-1616), Taming of the Shrew)*

13. His **house (DO)**, his **home (DO)**, his **heritage (DO)**, his **lands (DO)**,
    He left without a sigh. *(Lord Byron (1788-1824), "Childe Harold's Pilgrimage")*

    Note: These lines of poetry invert the sentence order. Consider, "He left his house, his home, his heritage, his lands without a sigh." The direct objects can be clearly seen.

14. On the tenth day of June, 1703, a boy on the topmast discovered **land (DO)**. *(Jonathan Swift (1667-1745), Gulliver's Travels)*

15. Have you turned **coward (PN)**?

16. This goodly frame, the earth, seems to me a sterile **promontory (PN)**. *(William Shakespeare (1564-1616), Hamlet)*

17. This southern tempest soon
    May change its **quarter (DO)** with the changing moon.
    (William Falconer (1732-1769), The Shipwreck)

18. Mr. Bletson arose and paid his **respects (DO)** to Colonel Everard. *(Sir Walter Scott (1771-1832), Woodstock)*

19. Escape seemed a desperate and impossible **adventure (PN)**. *(Sir Walter Scott (1771-1832), Quentin Durward)*

20. Here I reign **king (PN)**.

21. She uttered a half-stifled **shriek (DO)**. *(Emma Robinson (1814-1890), Caesar Borgia)*

22. The sailors joined his **prayer (DO)** in silent thought. *(William Falconer (1732-1769), The Shipwreck)*

23. We have been lamenting your **absence (DO)**.

24. This spark will prove a raging **fire (PN)**. *(William Shakespeare (1564-1616), King Henry VI)*

Chapter 45: Pronoun as Predicate Nominative

Students were instructed to label the the subjects with S and the predicate nominatives with PN. Not every subject has a predicate nominative.

1. "**Who (S)**'s there?" "**It (S)** 's **I (PN)**!"

2. **I (S)** wish to see Mr. Smith. Are **you (S)** **he (PN)**?

3. "Do **you (S)** know John Anson? "Yes, **that (S)** 's **he (PN)**!"

4. **(You) (S)** See that poor fellow! **I (S)** shouldn't like to be **he (PN)**.

5. **I (S)** asked to see your sons. Are **these (S)** **they (PN)**?"
   "Yes, **these (S)** are **they (PN)**. Shall **I (S)** tell you their names?"

6. "**It (S)** 's **she (PN)**! There **she (S)** is!" cried the **children (S)** eagerly.

7. Yes, **it (S)** was **he (PN)**, — the famous admiral.

8. **I (S)** wish **it (S)** hadn't been **I (PN)** that broke the window.

9. If **that (S)** is the rich Mrs. Blank, **I (S)** shouldn't like to be **she (PN)**.

10. "**Who (S)** 's there?" "**It (S)** 's **we (PN)**." "**Who (S)** are **you (PN)**?"

11. The best **grammarians (S)** in the village are **we (PN)** four girls.

Chapter 46: Analysis: Predicate Nominative and Predicate Adjective

Students were instructed to analyze sentences 1-4 and 6-15. Optional sentences 5 and 16-24 are included and answers shown below. Conjunctions were not mentioned, but are identified here with (C).

1. (With how sad steps) (**Adv**), (O Moon) (**Adj**), <u>thou</u> | <u>climb'st</u> the (**Adj**) sky (**DO**)! *(Sir Philip Sidney (1554-1586), "Astrophel and Stella")*

2. The (**Adj**) <u>landscape</u> | <u>was</u> a (**Adj**) forest (**PN**) wide (**Adj**) and (**C**) bare (**Adj**). *(John Dryden (1631-1700), "Palamon and Arcite," a poem retelling the "A Knight's Tale")*

3. Here (**Adv**) the (**Adj**) <u>Albanian</u> | proudly (**Adv**) <u>treads</u> the (**Adj**) ground (**DO**). *(Lord Byron (1788-1824), "Childe Harold's Pilgrimage")*

4. (*You*) | <u>Wing</u> thy (**Adj**) flight (**DO**) (from hence) (**Adv phrase**) (on the morrow) (**Adv phrase**). *(Sir Walter Scott (1771-1832), Woodstock)*

5. <u>It</u> | <u>was</u> a (**Adj**) wild (**Adj**) and (**Conjunction**) strange (**Adj**) retreat, (**PN**)
   [As (**Adv**) e'er (**Adv**) <u>was trod</u> (by outlaw's feet). (**Adv phrase**)] (adjective clause modifying *retreat*)
   (Sir Walter Scott (1771-1832), "Lady of the Lake")*

6. <u>Honor</u> | <u>is</u> the (**Adj**) subject (**PN**) (of my story) (**Adj phrase**). *(William Shakespeare (1564-1616), Julius Caesar)*

7. <u>I</u> alone (**Adj**) | <u>became</u> their (**Adj**) prisoner (**PN**). *(William Shakespeare (1564-1616), Hamlet)*

8. A (**Adj**) strange (**Adj**) group (**PN**) <u>we</u> | <u>were</u>. *"A strange group" is part of the predicate, but precedes the subject. Students may identify "group" as the subject and "we" as the predicate nominative. This would be acceptable.*

9. The (**Adj**) mountain (**Adj**) <u>mist</u> | <u>took</u> form (**DO**) and (**C**) limb, (**DO**)
   (Of (noontide hag) or (goblin grim)) (**Adj phrase modifying "form" and "limb"**).
   (Sir Walter Scott (1771-1832), "Lady of the Lake")

10. The (**Adj**) family (**Adj**) <u>specialties</u> | <u>were</u> health (**PN**), (good (**Adj**) humor) (**PN**), and (**C**) vivacity (**PN**). *(Henry Kingsley (1830-1876), The Hillyars and the Burtons: A Story of Two Families)*

11. The (**Adj**) deep (**Adj**) war-drum's (**Adj**) <u>sound</u> | <u>announced</u> the (**Adj**) close (**DO**) (of day) (**Adj**). *(Lord Byron (1788-1824), "Childe Harold's Pilgrimage")*

12. <u>You</u> | <u>seem</u> a (**Adj**) sober (**Adj**) ancient (**Adj**) gentleman (**PN**). *(William Shakespeare (1564-1616), Taming of the Shrew)*

13. His (**Adj**) house (**DO**), his (**Adj**) home (**DO**), his (**Adj**) heritage (**DO**), his (**Adj**) lands, (**DO**)
    <u>He</u> | <u>left</u> (without a sigh) (**Adv**). *(Lord Byron (1788-1824), "Childe Harold's Pilgrimage")*

14. {(On the tenth day) (of June, 1703) (**Adj phrase modifying *day*)}** (**Adv phrase modifying *discovered***), a <u>boy</u> (on the topmast) (**Adj**) | <u>discovered</u> land (**DO**). *(Jonathan Swift (1667-1745), Gulliver's Travels)*

15. <u>Have</u> <u>you</u> | <u>turned</u> coward (**PN**)?

16. This (**Adj**) goodly (**Adj**) <u>frame</u>, (the earth) (**Adj-appositive**), | <u>seems</u> (to me) (**Adv**) a (**Adj**) sterile (**Adj**) promontory (**PN**). *(William Shakespeare (1564-1616), Hamlet)*

17. This (**Adj**) southern (**Adj**) <u>tempest</u> | soon (**Adv**)
    <u>May change</u> its (**Adj**) quarter (**DO**) (with the changing moon) (**Adv**).

(William Falconer (1732-1769), "The Shipwreck")

18. <u>Mr. Bletson</u> | <u>arose</u> and (**C**) <u>paid</u> his (**Adj**) respects (**DO**) (to Colonel Everard) (**IO**). *(Sir Walter Scott (1771-1832), Woodstock)*

19. <u>Escape</u> | <u>seemed</u> a (**Adj**) desperate (**Adj**) and (**C**) impossible (**Adj**) adventure (**PN**). *(Sir Walter Scott (1771-1832), Quentin Durward)*

20. Here (**Adv**) <u>I</u> | <u>reign</u> king (**PN**).

21. <u>She</u> | <u>uttered</u> a (**Adj**) half-stifled (**Adj**) shriek (**DO**). *(Emma Robinson (1814-1890), Caesar Borgia)*

22. The (**Adj**) <u>sailors</u> | <u>joined</u> his (**Adj**) prayer (**DO**) (in silent thought) (**Adv**). *(William Falconer (1732-1769), "The Shipwreck")*

23. <u>We</u> | <u>have been lamenting</u> your (**Adj**) absence (**DO**).

24. This (**Adj**) <u>spark</u> | <u>will prove</u> a (**Adj**) raging (**Adj**) fire (**PN**). *(William Shakespeare (1564-1616), King Henry VI)*

Chapter 47: Simple Subject and Compound Subject

I.

Check to be sure that students have properly paired the substantives with conjunctions and used as a compound subject. Answers will vary.

II.

Students were instructed to divide the complete subject and predicate with a vertical line. The compound subjects should be underlined and the conjunction circled (shown in bold here).

1. <u>Sorrow</u> **and** <u>sadness</u> | sat upon every face. *(Thomas Evans (1798-1868)*, Life of Gilbert Latey)

2. These <u>terrors</u> **and** <u>apprehensions</u> of the people | led them into a thousand weak, foolish, and wicked things. *(Daniel Defoe (1660-1731)*, A Journal of the Plague Year)

3. <u>Tears</u> | lie in him, **and** consuming <u>fire</u>. *(Thomas Carlyle (1795-1881)*, Robert Burns)

4. <u>Homer</u> **and** <u>Socrates</u> **and** the Christian <u>apostles</u> | belong to old days. *(Thomas Carlyle (1795-1881)*, Robert Burns)

5. My childish <u>years</u> **and** his hasty <u>departure</u> | prevented me from enjoying the full benefit of his lessons. *(Edward Gibbon (1737-1794)*, Memoirs of My Life)

6. Everywhere new <u>pleasures</u>, new <u>interests</u> | awaited me. *(Thomas Moore (1779-1852)*, The Epicurean)

7. His <u>integrity</u> **and** <u>benevolence</u> | are equal to his learning. *(Samuel Johnson (1709-1784)*, The History of Rasselas, Prince of Abyssinia: A Tale)

8. **Both** <u>saw</u> **and** <u>axe</u> | were plied vigorously.

9. **Neither** <u>Turk</u> **nor** <u>Tartar</u> | can frighten him.

10. The <u>duke</u> **and** his <u>senators</u> | left the court.

11. **Either** <u>Rome</u> **or** <u>Carthage</u> | must perish.

12. Her varying <u>color</u>, her clouded <u>brow</u>, her thoughtful yet wandering <u>eye</u>, so different from the usual open, bland expression of her countenance, | plainly indicated the state of her feelings. *(Susan Ferrier (1782-1854)*, The Inheritance) *Note: Students may have circled* yet, *however this conjunction does not link together compound subjects. It links the multiple adjectives for eye.*

13. <u>Moss</u> **and** <u>clay</u> **and** <u>leaves</u> | combined
    To fence each crevice from the wind.
    (Sir Walter Scott (1771-1832), "Lady of the Lake")

14. <u>Tower</u> **and** <u>town</u> **and** <u>cottage</u> |
    Have heard the trumpet's blast.
    (Lord Thomas Macaulay (1800-1859), "Horatius")

15. The <u>horsemen</u> **and** the <u>footmen</u> |
    Are pouring in amain
    From many a stately marketplace,
    From many a fruitful plain.
    (Lord Thomas Macaulay (1800-1859), "Horatius")

16. <u>Groans</u> **and** <u>shrieks</u> | filled the air. *(William Shakespeare (1564-1616)*, adapted from Macbeth)

17. The <u>walls</u> **and** <u>gates</u> of the town | were strongly guarded.

18. <u>Chariots</u>, <u>horses</u>, <u>men</u>, | were huddled together.

Chapter 48: Simple Predicate and Compound Predicate

I.
Students were instructed to divide the complete subject and predicate with a vertical line. The compound predicates should be underlined and the conjunction circled (shown in bold here).

1. The wakeful bloodhound | <u>rose</u>, **and** <u>shook</u> his hide.

2. They | <u>clambered</u> through the cavity, **and** <u>began</u> to go down on the other side.

3. During this time, I | **neither** <u>saw</u> **nor** <u>heard</u> of Alethe.

4. The blackbird amid leafy trees,
    The lark above the hill, |
    <u>Let</u> loose their carols when they please,
    <u>Are</u> quiet when they will.
    (William Wordsworth (1770-1850), "The Fountain")

5. She | immediately <u>scrambled</u> across the fence **and** <u>walked</u> away. *(Jane Austen (1775-1817), Mansfield Park)*

6. John | <u>made</u> no further reply, **but** <u>left</u> the room sullenly, whistling as he went. *(Maria Edgeworth (1768-1849),* The Patronage*) Note: "Whistling" is a participle describing John and is not a compound predicate.*

7. I | <u>dressed</u> myself, <u>took</u> my hat and gloves, **and** <u>lingered</u> a little in the room. *(Thomas De Quincey (1785-1859),* Confessions of an English Opium-Eater*)*

8. The sun | <u>had</u> just <u>risen</u> **and**, from the summit of the Arabian hills, <u>was pouring</u> down his beams into that vast valley of waters. *(Thomas Moore (1779-1852),* The Epicurean*)*

9. They | <u>kept</u> up the Christmas carol, <u>sent</u> true-love knots on Valentine morning, <u>ate</u> pancakes on Shrovetide, <u>showed</u> their wit on the first of April, **and** religiously <u>cracked</u> nuts on Michaelmas eve. *(Oliver Goldsmith (1730-1774),* The Vicar of Wakefield*)*

II.
Check to see that students properly used the pairs of verbs in a compound predicate joined by a conjunction. Answers will vary.

Chapter 48: Review Exercises

I.

Students need to list the compound subjects or predicates that they composed in chapter 25, Exercises II and III. Answers will vary.

II.

Students were instructed to analyze the following sentences.

1. The (**Adj**) <u>wind</u> | <u>was</u> either (**C**) too (**Adv**) light (**PA**) or (**C**) <u>blew</u> (from the wrong quarter) (**Adv**).

2. They | <u>obey</u> their (**Adj**) guide (**DO**), and (**C**) <u>are</u> happy (**Adj**). *(Samuel Johnson (1709-1784),* The History of Rasselas, Prince of Abyssinia: A Tale*)*

3. The (**Adj**) <u>stranger</u> | neither (**C**) <u>spoke</u> nor (**C**) <u>read</u> English (**DO**).

4. The (**Adj**) <u>water</u> | <u>looked</u> muddy (**PA**) and (**C**) <u>tasted</u> brackish (**PA**), but (**C**) <u>was</u> eagerly (**Adv**) <u>drunk</u> (by the travelers) (**Adv**).

5. The (**Adj**) <u>watchman</u> | <u>was</u> sleepy (**Adj**), but (**C**) <u>struggled</u> (against his drowsiness) (Adv).

6. The (**Adj**) <u>fox</u> | <u>was caught</u>, but (**C**) <u>escaped</u>.

7. The (**Adj**) <u>bear</u> | <u>growled</u> fiercely (**Adv**), but (**C**) <u>did</u> not (**Adv**) <u>touch</u> the (**Adj**) boy (**DO**).

8. The (**Adj**) <u>sails</u> | <u>were drying</u>, and (**C**) <u>flapped</u> lazily (**Adv**) (against the mast) (**Adv**). *(Charles Lever (1806-1872),* Harry Lorrequer*)*

9. The (**Adj**) <u>ladies</u> and (**C**) <u>gentlemen</u> | <u>were inclined</u> (to sneer) (**Adv**), and (**C**) <u>were giggling</u> audibly (**Adv**). *Note: "To sneer" is an infinitive modifying the verb, which students will study in chapter 127. Students may be unable to identify "to sneer" as an adverbial modifier at this point, which is fine. (William Makepeace Thackeray (1811-1863),* The Tremendous Adventures of Major Gahagan *)*

10. (From the first) (**Adv**), <u>Miss Rice</u> | <u>was interested</u> (in her servant) (**Adv**), and (**C**) <u>encouraged</u> her (**Adj**) confidences (**DO**). *(George Moore (1852-1933),* Esther Waters: an English Story*)*

11. He | <u>jumped</u> (into the gondola) (**Adv**) and (**C**) <u>was carried</u> away (**Adv**) (through the silence (**Adv**) (of the night) (**Adj phrase modifying** *silence*)). *(William Black (1841-1898),* Sunset*)*

12. She | <u>grew</u> pale (**PA**) herself (**Adj**) and (**C**) <u>dropped</u> his (**Adj**) hand (**DO**) suddenly (**Adv**). *Note: "Herself" is an intensive pronoun and may be regarded as an appositive, a modifier of the subject "she." Students will study self-pronouns in chapter 87 and may not be able to identify it now.*

13. <u>Reuben</u> | <u>came</u> in (**Adv**) hurriedly (**Adv**) and (**C**) <u>nodded</u> a (**Adj**) goodbye (**DO**) (to all (**Adv**) (of us) (**Adj modifying** *all*)).

14. Gravely (**Adv**) <u>he</u> | <u>greets</u> each (**Adj**) city (**Adj**) sire (**DO**),
    <u>Commends</u> each (**Adj**) pageant's (**Adj**) quaint (**Adj**) attire (**DO**),
    <u>Gives</u> (to the dancers) (**IO**) thanks (**DO**) aloud (**Adv**),
    And (**C**) <u>smiles</u> and (**C**) <u>nods</u> (upon the crowd) (**Adv**).
    (Sir Walter Scott (1771-1832), "Lady of the Lake")

15. <u>Flesh</u> and (**C**) <u>blood</u> | <u>could</u> not (**Adv**) <u>endure</u> such (**Adj**) hardships (**DO**).

Chapter 49: Clauses — Compound Sentences

Brackets are shown around the clauses and conjunctions are underlined. Point out to students that some authors choose to use a comma (sentence 4) or dashes (sentence 7) rather than a conjunction to separate clauses. Encourage students to study carefully the use of the semi-colon and comma in sentence 5.

1. [The door opened], **and** [the two men came out].

2. [They seemed mere machines], **and** [all their thoughts were employed in the care of their horses]. *(Oliver Goldsmith (1730-1774), The Bee, A Collection of Essays)*

3. [The neighbors stared and sighed], **yet** [they blessed the lad]. *(James Beattie (1735-1803), "The Minstrel")*

4. [Thy heart is sad], [thy home is far away]. *(Thomas Campbell (1777-1844), "The Pleasures of Hope")*

5. [Days and weeks slide imperceptibly away]; [November is just at hand], **and** [the half of it will soon be over]. *(William Cowper (1731-1800), "Letters")*

6. [Pass beneath the archway into the court], **and** [the sixteenth century closes around you].

7. [The ocean has its ebbings]--[so has grief]. *(Thomas Campbell (1777-1844), "Theodric")*

8. [Art thou here], **or** [is it but a dream]?

9. [The robins are not good solo singers], **but** [their chorus is unrivaled]. *(James Russell Lowell (1819-1891),"My Garden Acquaintance")*

10. [Summer was now coming on with hasty steps], **and** [my seventeenth birthday was fast approaching]. *(Thomas De Quincey (1785-1859), Confessions of an English Opium-Eater)*

11. [The night had been heavy and lowering], **but** [towards the morning it had changed to a slight frost], **and** [the ground and the trees were now covered with rime]. *(Thomas De Quincey (1785-1859), Confessions of an English Opium-Eater)*

12. [The war-pipes ceased], **but** [lake and hill
    Were busy with their echoes still].
    (Sir Walter Scott (1771-1832), "Lady of the Lake")

13. [St. Agnes' Eve — ah, bitter chill it was]!
    [The owl, for all his feathers, was a-cold];
    [The hare limped trembling through the frozen grass],
    And [silent was the flock in woolly fold].
    (John Keats (1795-1821), "The Eve of St. Agnes")

Chapter 50: Complex Sentences — Adverbial Clauses

I.

The main clause is underlined once and the subordinate clause is underlined twice. Adverbs or conjunctions are labeled.

1. King Robert was silent **when (Adv)** he heard this story. *(Sir Walter Scott (1771-1832),* Tales of a Grandfather*)*

2. He laughed **till (Adv)** the tears ran down his face.

3. **When (Adv)** the Arabs saw themselves out of danger, they slackened their pace.

4. We advance in freedom **as (Adv)** we advance in years.

5. **When (Adv)** I came back I resolved to settle in London.

6. **As (Adv)** he approached the stream, his heart began to thump.

7. He struggled on, **though (C)** he was very tired.

8. I consent **because (C)** you wish it.

9. Dr. Acton came down **while (Adv)** I was there.

10. We drove along through a beautiful country **till (Adv)** at length we came to the brow of a steep hill.

11. **As (Adv)** we grow old, our sense of the value of time becomes vivid.

12. **Just when (Adv)** the oak leaves first looked reddish, the whole tribe of finches burst forth in songs from every bough.

13. Jason and the bull wrestled **until (Adv)** the monster fell groveling on his knees.

14. **If (C)** any dispute arises, they apply to him for the decision.

15. **If (C)** this is no violent exercise, I am much mistaken.

16. Tell me the facts, **since (C)** you know them.

II.

Students were instructed to analyze the sentences in Exercise I.

1. (King Robert) **(S)** was **(V)** silent **(PA)** [when **(Adv)** he **(S)** heard **(V)** this **(Adj)** story **(DO)**] (**Adverbial clause** modifying *was*). *(Sir Walter Scott (1771-1832),* Tales of a Grandfather*)*

2. He **(S)** laughed **(V)** [till **(Adv)** the **(Adj)** tears **(S)** ran **(V)** (down his face) **(Adv phrase)**] (**Adverbial clause**).

3. [When **(Adv)** the **(Adj)** Arabs **(S)** saw **(V)** themselves **(DO)** (out of danger) **(Adj)**,] (**Adverbial clause** modifying *slackened*) they **(S)** slackened **(V)** their **(Adj)** pace **(DO)**.

4. We **(S)** advance **(V)** (in freedom) **(Adv)** [as we advance in years] (**Adverbial clause** modifying *advance*).

5. [When **(Adv)** I **(S)** came **(V)** back **(Adv)**] (**adverbial clause** modifying *resolved*) I **(S)** resolved **(V)** (to settle) ***(infinitive-Adv modifier)** (in London) (**Adv phrase** modifying *to settle*).

6. [As (**Adv**) he (**S**) approached (**V**) the (**Adj**) stream (**DO**)], (**Adverbial clause modifying** *began*) his (**Adj**) heart (**S**) began (**V**) (to thump)* (**infinitive-Adv modifier**).

7. He(**S**) struggled (**V**) on (**Adv**), [though (**C**) he (**S**) was (**V**) very (**Adv**) tired (**PA**)]. (**adverbial clause modifying** *struggled*)

8. I (**S**) consent (**V**) [because you wish it]. (**Adverbial clause modifying** *consent*)

9. (Dr. Acton) (**S**) came (**V**) down (**Adv**) [while (**Adv**) I (**S**) was (**V**) there (**Adv**)]. (**Adverbial clause modifying** *came*)

10. We (**S**) drove (**V**) along (**Adv**) (through a beautiful country) (**Adv prep phrase**) [till (**Adv**) (at length) (**Adv prep phrase**) we (**S**) came (**V**) ((to the brow) (**Adv prep phrase**) (of a steep hill) (**Adj prep phrase modifying the obj of prep** *brow*))]. (**Adverbial clause modifying** *drove*)

11. [As (**Adv**) we (**S**) grow (**V**) old (**PA**)], (**Adverbial clause modifying** *becomes*) our (**Adj**) sense (**S**) (of the value) (**Adj modifying** *sense*) (of time) (**Adj modifying** *time*)) becomes (**V**) vivid (**PA**).

12. [Just (**Adv**) when (**Adv**) the (**Adj**) oak (**Adj**) leaves (**S**) first (**Adv**) looked (**V**) reddish (**PA**)] (**Adverbial clause modifying** *burst*), the (**Adj**) whole (**Adj**) tribe (**S**) (of finches) (**Adj**) burst (**V**) forth (**Adv**) (in songs) (**Adv phrase**) (from every bough) (**Adv phrase**).

13. Jason (**Compound S**) and (**C**) the (**Adj**) bull (**Compound S**) wrestled (**V**) [until (**Adv**) the (**Adj**) monster (**S**) fell (**V**) groveling (**Present participle**)* (on his knees)]. (**Adverbial clause modifying** *wrestled*)

14. [If (**C**) any (**Adj**) dispute (**S**) arises (**V**)] (**Adverbial clause modifying** *apply*), they (**S**) apply (**V**) (to him) (**Adv phrase**) (for the decision) (**Adv phrase**).

15. [If (**C**) this (**S**) is (**V**) no (**Adv**) violent (**Adj**) exercise (**PN**)], (**Adverbial clause modifying** *am mistaken*) I (**S**) am (**V**) much (**Adv**) mistaken (**V**).

16. *(You)* (**S**) Tell (**V**) me (**IO**) the (**Adj**) facts (**DO**) , [since (**Adv**) you (**S**) know (**V**) them (**DO**)].

*Students have not studied infinitives or participles yet, so may not know how to identify these words.

Chapter 51: Relative Pronouns

I.

The main clause is underlined once; the subordinate clause is underlined twice. Subjects and predicates are labeled.

1. **Harry (S) has lost (V)** a knife   *which* **(S) belongs (V)** to me.
2. **I (S) have (V)** a friend   *whose* **name (S) is (V)** Arthur.
3. The **girl (S)** *whom* **you (S) saw (V)**   **is (V)** my sister.
4. **(You) (S) Tell (V)** me the news   *that* **you (S) have heard (V)**.

Students were instructed to identify if the relative pronoun is the subject, object, or genitive.

1. Subject
2. Genitive
3. Object
4. Object

II.

Students were instructed to supply the relative pronoun and circle its antecedent, which is bolded here. Answers may vary.

1. The **house**   which   stands yonder belongs to Colonel Carton.
2. Are you the **man**   who   saved my daughter from drowning?
3. The sailor's wife gazed at the stately **ship**   which   was taking her husband away from her.
4. A young **farmer**,   whose   name was Judkins, was the first to enlist.
5. **Nothing**   that   you can do will help me.
6. The **horses**   which   belong to the squire are famous trotters.
7. James Adams is the strongest **man**   that   I have ever seen.
8. My **friend**,   whom   we had overtaken on his way down town, greeted us cheerfully.
9. Behold the **man**   whom   the king delighteth to honor! *(Esther 6:9, adapted from King James Version)*
10. That is the **captain**   whose   ship was wrecked last December.

III.

Students were instructed to circle the relative pronouns (bolded here) and drawn an arrow to the antecedent (shown in italics after the pronoun). The main clause is underlined once, the subordinate clause(s) twice. Subjects and verbs are labeled.

1. A sharp rattle **(S)** (was heard) **(V)** on the window,   **which** *(rattle)* **(S)** made **(V)** [the children **(S)** jump **(V)**].
2. The small torch **(S)** **that** *(torch)* he **(S)** held **(V)**   sent **(V)** forth a radiance   by **which** *(radiance)* suddenly the whole surface **(S)** of the desert (was illuminated) **(V)**. *(Thomas Moore (1779-1852), The Epicurean)*
3. He **(S)** **that** *(he)* **(S)** has **(V)** most time   has **(V)** none to lose. *(Benjamin Disraeli (1804-1881))*
4. Gray rocks **(S)** peeped **(V)** from amidst the lichens and creeping plants   **which (S)** *(lichens and plants)* covered **(V)** them as with a garment of many colors. *(Susan Ferrier (1782-1854), The Inheritance)*
5. The enclosed fields **(S)**, **which** *(fields)* **(S)** were **(V)** generally forty feet square, resembled **(V)** so many beds of flowers. *(Jonathan Swift (1667-1745), Gulliver's Travels)*

6. They **(S)** **that** (*they*) **(S)** reverence **(V)** too much old times are **(V)** but a scorn to the new. *(Francis Bacon (1561-1626), "Of Innovations")*

7. The morning **(S)** came **(V)** **which** (*morning*) **(S)** was **(V)** to launch me into the world, and from **which** (*morning*) my whole succeeding life **(S)** has **(V)**, in many important points, taken **(V)** its coloring. *(Thomas De Quincey (1785-1859),* Confessions of an English Opium-Eater*)*

8. Ten guineas **(S)**, added to about two **which** (*two*) I **(S)** (had remaining) **(V)** from my pocket money, seemed **(V)** to me sufficient for an indefinite length of time. *(Thomas De Quincey (1785-1859),* Confessions of an English Opium-Eater*)*

9. He **(S)** is **(V)** the freeman **whom** (*freeman*) the truth **(S)** makes **(V)** free. *(William Cowper (1731-1800),* The Task*)*

10. There was **(V)** one philosopher **(S)** **who** (*philosopher*) **(S)** chose **(V)** to live in a tub. *(Robert Southey (1774-1843),* The Doctor*)*

11. Conquerors **(S)** are **(V)** a class of men with **whom** (*class*), for the most part, the world **(S)** could **(V)** well dispense **(V)**. *(Thomas Carlyle (1795-1881),* Robert Burns*)*

12. The light **(S)** came **(V)** from a lamp **that** (*lamp*) **(S)** burned **(V)** brightly on the table.

13. The sluggish stream **(S)** through **which** (*stream*) we **(S)** moved **(V)** yielded **(V)** sullenly to the oar. *(Thomas Moore (1779-1852),* The Epicurean*)*

14. The place **(S)** from **which** (*place*) the light **(S)** proceeded **(V)** was **(V)** a small chapel.

15. The warriors **(S)** went **(V)** into battle clad in complete armor, **which** (*armor*) **(S)** covered them from top to toe. *(Sir Walter Scott (1771-1832),* History of Scotland*)*

16. She **(S)** seemed **(V)** as happy as a wave
    That (*wave*) **(S)** dances **(V)** on the sea.
    (William Wordsworth (1770-1850), "The Two April Mornings")

17. He **(S)** sang **(V)** out a long, loud, and canorous peal of laughter, **that** (*peal*) **(S)** (might have wakened) **(V)** the Seven Sleepers. *(Thomas De Quincey (1785-1859),* Confessions of an English Opium-Eater*)*

18. Thou **(S)** hadst **(V)** a voice **whose** (*voice*) sound **(S)** was **(V)** like the sea. *(William Wordsworth (1770-1850), "Sonnet to Milton")*

19. Many of Douglas's followers **(S)** (were slain) **(V)** in the battle in **which** (*battle*) he **(S)** himself fell **(V)**. *(Sir Walter Scott (1771-1832),* Tales of a Grandfather*)*

Chapter 52: Adjective Clauses

I.

Students were instructed to underline the adjective clauses and circle (bolded here) the substantive that each describes or limits.

1. The careless messenger lost the **letter** <u>which had been entrusted to him</u>.
2. The merchant gave the **sailor** <u>who rescued him</u> a thousand dollars.
3. The officer selected seven men, **veterans** <u>whose courage had often been tested</u>.
4. My traveling companion was an old **gentleman** <u>whom I had met in Paris</u>.
5. The **castle** <u>where I was born</u> lies in ruins.
6. Alas! the **spring** <u>which had watered this oasis</u> was dried up.
7. The **time** <u>that you have wasted</u> would have made an industrious man rich.
8. A strange **fish**, <u>which had wings</u>, was this day captured by the seamen.
9. This happened at a **time** <u>when prices were high</u>.

II.

Students were instructed to analyze the sentences from Exercise I, reproduced below.

1. <u>The (**Adj**) careless (**Adj**) messenger (**S**) lost (**V**) the (**Adj**) letter (**DO**) [which (**S**) (had been entrusted) (**V**) (to him) (**Adv phrase**)]</u>. (**Adjective clause modifying** *letter*)
2. <u>The (**Adj**) merchant (**S**) gave (**V**) the (**Adj**) sailor (**IO**) [who (**S**) rescued (**V**) him (**DO**)]</u> (**Adjective clause modifying** *sailor*) <u>a (**Adj**) thousand (**Adj**) dollars (**DO**)</u>.
3. <u>The (**Adj**) officer(**S**) selected (**V**) seven (**Adj**) men (**DO**), veterans (**Appositive adjective**) [whose (**Adj**) courage (**S**) (had (often) (**Adv**) been tested) (**V**)]</u>. (**Adjective clause modifying** *veterans*)
4. <u>My (**Adj**) traveling (**Adj**) companion (**S**) was (**V**) an (**Adj**) old (**Adj**) gentleman (**PN**) [whom (**DO**) I (**S**) (had met) (**V**) (in Paris) (**Adv**)]</u>. (**Adjective clause modifying** *gentleman*)
5. <u>The (**Adj**) castle (**S**) [where (**Adv**) I (**S**) (was born) (**V**)]</u> (**Adjective clause modifying** *castle*) <u>lies (**V**) (in ruins) (**Adv**)</u>.
6. Alas! (**Interjection**) <u>the (**Adj**) spring (**S**) [which (**S**) (had watered) (**V**) this (**Adj**) oasis (**DO**)]</u> (**Adjective clause modifying** *spring*) <u>(was dried) (**V**) up (**Adv**)</u>.
7. <u>The (**Adj**) time (**S**) [that (**DO**) you (**S**) (have wasted) (**V**)]</u> (**Adjective clause modifying** *time*) <u>(would have made) (**V**) an (**Adj**) industrious (**Adj**) man (**DO**) rich (**Adj**)</u>.
8. <u>A (**Adj**) strange (**Adj**) fish (**S**), [which (**S**) had (**V**) wings (**DO**)]</u>, (**Adjective clause modifying** *fish*) <u>was (**V**) (this day) (**Adv phrase**) captured (**V**) (by the seamen) (**Adv**)</u>.
9. <u>This (**S**) happened (**V**) (at a time) (**Adv phrase**) [when (**Adv**) prices (**S**) were (**V**) high (**PA**)]</u>. (**Adjective clause modifying** *time*)

Chapter 53: Noun Clauses

I.
Check for sentences that use nouns as subjects, direct objects, predicate nominatives, and appositives. Answers will vary.

II.
The student was instructed to underline noun clauses and label them.

1. That some mistake had occurred (**S**) was evident.

2. That republics are ungrateful (**S**) is a common saying.

3. That fire burns (**S**) is one of the first lessons of childhood.

4. That the fever was spreading (**S**) became only too apparent.

5. I know that he has received a letter (**DO**).

6. I wish that you would study harder (**DO**).

7. From that moment I resolved that I would stay in the town (**DO**).

8. Bassanio confessed to Portia that he had no fortune (**DO**). (*Charles and Mary Lamb's* Tales from Shakespeare, *"Merchant of Venice"*)

9. My opinion is that this story is false (**PN**).

10. His decision was that the castle should be surrendered (**PN**).

11. The saying that the third time never fails (**App**) is old.

12. The lesson that work is necessary (**App**) is learned early.

III.
Students were instructed to identify sentences as compound or complex, draw brackets around its clauses, and label the clauses.

1.	**complex**	All the birds began to sing [when the sun rose]. (**Adv**)
2.	**complex**	The house stands [where three roads meet]. (**Adv**)
3.	**complex**	He worked hard all his life [that he might enjoy leisure in his old age]. (**Adv**)
4.	**complex**	The earth caved in upon the miner [so that he was completely buried]. (**Adv**)
5.	**complex**	I will give you ten cents [if you will hold my horse]. (**Adv**)
6.	**complex**	The wanderer trudged on, [though he was very tired]. (**Adv**)
7.	**complex**	The only obstacle to our sailing was [that we had not yet completed our complement of men]. (**N-PN**) *(Frederick Marryat (1792-1848),* Peter Simple*)*
8.	**compound**	[Spring had come again, after a long, wet winter,] and [every orchard hollow blushed once more with apple blossoms]. *(Henry Kingsley (1830-1876),* The Recollections of Geoffry Hamlyn) *Note: Compound sentences are two independent clauses, not adjective or adverbial.*
9.	**complex**	A great stone [that I happened to find by the seashore] (**N-appositive**) served me for an anchor. *(Jonathan Swift (1667-1745),* Gulliver's Travels*)*
10.	**complex**	[If you will go over] (**Adv**), I will follow you.

11. **complex**   He would give the most unpalatable advice, [if need were]. (**Adv**) *(Elizabeth Gaskell (1810-1865), A Dark Night's Work)*

12. **complex**   The first thing [that made its appearance] (**N-Appositive**) was an enormous ham. *(Washington Irving (1783-1859), Tales of a Traveler)*

13. **complex**   [As Pen followed his companion up the creaking old stair] (**Adv**), his knees trembled under him. *(William Makepeace Thackeray (1811-1863), History of Pendennis)*

14. **compound**   [Two old ladies in black came out of the old-fashioned garden]; [they walked towards a seat and sat down in the autumn landscape]. *Note: Compound sentences are two independent clauses, not adjective or adverbial.*

15. **complex**   The brigand drew a stiletto and rushed upon his adversary. The man eluded the blow and defended himself with his pistol, [which had a spring bayonet]. (**Adj**) *(Washington Irving (1783-1859), Tales of a Traveler)*

16. **complex**   [In the midst of this strait, and hard by a group of rocks called the Hen and Chickens] (**Adv**), there lay the wreck of a vessel [which had been entangled in the whirlpools and stranded during a storm]. (**Adj**) *(Washington Irving (1783-1859), Tales of a Traveler)*

Chapter 54: The Same Word as Different Parts of Speech

I.

1. We sit in the warm shade and feel right well
   How the sap creeps up and the blossoms *swell*.
   verb-tells what blossoms do
   (James Russell Lowell (1819-1891), "Vision of Sir Launfal")

2. Like the *swell* of some sweet tune
   Morning rises into noon,
   May glides onward into June.
   noun-names a thing
   (Henry Wadsworth Longfellow (1807-1882), "Maidenhood")

3. Use your chances while they *last*.
   verb-tells what chances do

4. Shoemaker, stick to your *last*.
   noun-names a thing
   (Expression comes from the Latin Sutor, ne ultra crepidam, *which means, "Shoemaker, no higher than the sandal," meaning, "Stick to your expertise." A* last *is the form shaped like a foot that shoemakers use in making and repairing shoes.)*

5. Down came squirrel, eager for his fare,
   Down came bonny blackbird, I declare!
   Little Bell gave each his honest *share*.
   noun-names a thing
   (Thomas Westwood (1814-1888), "Little Bell")

6. Not what we give, but what we *share*,
   For the gift without the giver is bare.
   verb-tells what we do
   (James Russell Lowell (1819-1891), "Vision of Sir Laufal")

7. Heaped in the hollows of the grove, the autumn leaves lie dead,
   They rustle to the eddying gust and to the rabbit's *tread*.
   noun-names a thing
   (William Cullen Bryant (1794-1878), "Death of the Flowers")

8. All that *tread* the globe
   Are but a handful to the tribes
   That slumber in its bosom.
   verb-tells what "all" do
   (William Cullen Bryant (1794-1878), "Thanatopsis")

9. But what shall I gain by young Arthur's *fall*?
   noun-names a thing
   (William Shakespeare (1564-1616), King John*)*

10. The woods decay, the woods decay and *fall*.
    verb-tells what the woods do
    (Alfred, Lord Tennyson (1809-1892), "Tithonus")

II.
Make sure that students have used each word as a noun and a verb. Answers will vary.

Chapter 55: Nouns and Adjectives

I.

Students were instructed to label the italicized words as noun (N) or adjective (Adj) and give reasons.

1. God gives sleep to the *bad* **(N)** in order that the *good* **(N)** may be undisturbed. *(Saadi Shirazi (1210-1291))*
   used as substantives (object of preposition and subject of verb)

2. Is thy news *good* **(Adj)** or *bad*? **(Adj)** *(William Shakespeare (1564-1616),* Romeo and Juliet*)*
   used as modifiers of substantive *news*

3. She shall be a high and *mighty* **(Adj)** queen. *(William Shakespeare (1564-1616),* Richard III*)*
   used as modifier of substantive *queen*

4. He hath put down the *mighty* **(N)** from their seats. *(Luke 1:52, King James Version)*
   used as substantive (direct object)

5. Alexander was a *mighty* **(Adj)** conqueror.
   used as modifier of substantive *conqueror*

6. Give us some *gold* **(N)**, good Timon! Hast thou more? *(William Shakespeare (1564-1616),* Timon of Athens*)*
   used as substantive (direct object)

7. Man wants but *little* **(N)** here below,
   "Nor wants that *little* **(N)** long." *(Oliver Goldsmith (1730-1774),* The Hermit*)*
   used as substantive (direct objects)

8. The fairy wore a *little* **(Adj)** red cap.
   used as modifier of substantive *cap*

9. I heard thee murmur tales of *iron* **(Adj)** wars. *(William Shakespeare (1564-1616),* Henry IV*)*
   used as modifier of substantive *wars*

10. Strike now, or else the *iron* **(N)** cools. *(William Shakespeare (1564-1616),* Henry VI*)*
    used as substantive (subject of verb)

11. Without haste, without rest.
    Lifting *better* **(N)** up to *best* **(N)**. *(Ralph Waldo Emerson (1803-1882))*
    used as substantives (objects)

12. You are a *better* **(Adj)** scholar than I.
    modifier of substantive *scholar*

13. I stand before you a *free* **(Adj)** man.
    modifier of substantive *man*

14. The Star Spangled Banner, O long may it wave
    O'er the land of the *free* **(N)** and the home of the *brave*! **(N)**
    (Francis Scott Key (1779-1843), "Star Spangled Banner")
    used as substantives (objects of the preposition)

15. Nature ne'er deserts the *wise* **(N)** and *pure*. **(N)**
    (Samuel Taylor Coleridge (1772-1834), "The Lime-Tree Bower My Prison")
    used as substantives (direct objects)

II.

Check that students wrote sentences using each word given as a noun and as an adjective. Answers will vary.

III.

Check that students wrote sentences using each word given as a noun and as an adjective. Answers will vary.

Chapter 56: Adjectives and Adverbs

Study the italicized words and write its part of speech (noun, adjective, adverb, or preposition) in the blank. Remember that the sense determines its usage.

1.	**preposition**	I must reach town *before* night.
2.	**adverb**	I have met you *before*.
3.	**adverb**	Is there anybody *within*?
4.	**preposition**	*Within* this half hour will he be asleep.
5.	**preposition**	The city stands on a hill *above* the harbor.
6.	**adverb**	The sun shines *above*; the waves are dancing.
7.	**preposition**	He went *by* the house at a great pace.
8.	**adverb**	He passed *by* on the other side.
9.	**preposition**	The horse was running *down* the road.
10.	**adverb**	The lion lay *down* in his lair.
11.	**adverb**	Come *quick*! We need your help at once.
12.	**adjective**	Elton was a *quick* and skillful workman.
13.	**noun**	This remark cuts me to the *quick*.
14.	**adjective**	*Hard* work cannot harm a healthy man.
15.	**adverb**	A healthy man can work *hard*.
16.	**adverb**	Jack rose *early*, for he meant to go a-fishing.

Chapter 57: Review: Structure of Sentences

There are no written exercises for this chapter.

Chapter 58: Form of Analysis

There are no written exercises for this chapter.

Chapter 59: Inflection

There are no written exercises for this chapter.

Chapter 60: Summary of Inflections

There are no written exercises for this chapter.

Chapter 61: Gender

I.

Students were instructed to circle all the pronouns (bolded below), label the gender of each (masculine with M, feminine with F, or neuter with N; if masculine or feminine, such as *their*, use M/F) and draw an arrow to the noun to which each refers (shown in parentheses).

1. The horse was injured in one of **his (M, horse)** hind legs.

2. Esther was going to see if **she (F, Esther)** could get some fresh eggs for **her (F, Esther)** mistress's breakfast before the shops closed. *(George Moore (1852-1933),* Esther Waters: an English Story*)*

3. All speech, even the commonest speech, has something of song in **it (N, speech)**. *(Thomas Carlyle (1795-1881),* The Hero as Poet*)*

4. Sam ran out to hold **his (M, Sam)** father's horse.

5. "Now, Doctor," cried the boys, "do tell **us (M, boys)** your adventures!"

6. Our English archers bent **their (M/F, archers)** bows,
   Their (M/F, archers) hearts were good and true,
   At the first flight of arrows sent,
   Full fourscore Scots **they (M/F, archers)** slew.
   (Author unknown, The Ballad of Chevy Chase*)*

7. The bridegroom stood dangling **his (M, bridegroom)** bonnet and plume. *(Sir Walter Scott (1771-1832), "Lochinvar")*

8. Emma was sitting in the midst of the children, telling **them (M/F, children)** a story; and **she (F, Emma)** came smiling towards Erne, holding out **her (F, Emma)** hand. *(Henry Kingsley (1830-1876),* The Hillyars and the Burtons: A Story of Two Families*)*

II.

Fill in each blank with a noun or a pronoun. Tell its gender, and give your reason.

1. The poet had written _his_ last song. **M**
2. _She_ swept the hearth and mended the fire. **F**
3. The old farmer sat in _his_ armchair. **M**
4. Tom lost _his_ knife; but Philip found _it_. **M, N**
5. Arthur and Kate studied _their_ lessons together. **M/F**
6. The Indian picked up a stone and threw _it_ at the bird. **N**
7. The tracks were so faint that _they_ could not be followed. **M/F**
8. My aunt has sold _her_ horse to _her_ cousin. **F, F**

Chapter 62: Special Rules of Gender, Part 1: Personification

Students were instructed to circle the pronouns that personify an object in the following selection. They are bolded below. There should be 15 identified.

This day the sun rose clear; we had a fine wind, and everything was bright and cheerful. I had now got my sea legs on, and was beginning to enter upon the regular duties of a sea life. About six bells, that is, three o'clock P.M., we saw a sail on our larboard bow. I was very desirous, like every new sailor, to speak to **her**. **She** came down to us, backed **her** main topsail, and the two vessels stood "head on," bowing and curveting at each other like a couple of war horses reined in by their riders. It was the first vessel that I had seen near, and I was surprised to find how much **she** rolled and pitched in so quiet a sea. **She** plunged **her** head into the sea, and then, **her** stern settling gradually down, **her** huge bows rose up, showing the bright copper, and **her** stern and breasthooks dripping, like old Neptune's locks, with the brine. **Her** decks were filled with passengers, who had come up at the cry of "Sail ho!" and who, by their dress and features, appeared to be Swiss and French emigrants. **She** hailed us at first in French, but receiving no answer, **she** tried us in English. **She** was the ship *La Carolina*, from Havre, for New York. We desired **her** to report the brig *Pilgrim*, from Boston, for the northwest coast of America, five days out. **She** then filled away and left us to plow on through our waste of waters.
-RICHARD HENRY DANA, JR.

Why are some objects and qualities regarded as masculine and others as feminine?

This is mostly by tradition, and is falling out of favor in modern culture, but nevertheless some objects, such as ships, continue to be personified.

Chapter 63: Special Rules of Gender, Part 2: Pronoun for Animals

Students were instructed to write sentences using pronouns with the correct gender. Check their sentences to be sure they followed instructions.

Chapter 64: Plural of Nouns

	SINGULAR	*PLURAL*
boy	boy	boys
girl	girl	girls
field	field	fields
street	street	streets
paper	paper	papers
book	book	books
pencil	pencil	pencils
brick	brick	bricks
bell	bell	bells
door	door	doors
hat	hat	hats
lesson	lesson	lessons
president	president	presidents
governor	governor	governors

	SINGULAR	*PLURAL*
fly	fly	flies
cry	cry	cries
reply	reply	replies
supply	supply	supplies
ally	ally	allies
remedy	remedy	remedies
subsidy	subsidy	subsidies

	Singular	*Plural*
toy	toy	toys
play	play	plays
alley	alley	alleys
donkey	donkey	donkeys
ray	ray	rays
dray	dray	drays
survey	survey	surveys

	Singular	*Plural*
calf	calf	calves
half	half	halves
loaf	loaf	loaves
knife	knife	knives
wife	wife	wives
life	life	lives

Compare your four lists, and see if you can frame a rule for the plural of:

(1) nouns that end in -y after a consonant,
Nouns ending in -y after a consonant are changed to plural by dropping the -y and adding -ies.

(2) nouns that end in -y after a vowel,
Nouns ending in -y after a vowel are changed to plural by adding -s.

(3) nouns like calf and knife.
Some nouns ending in the /f/ sound are changed to plural by dropping the f and adding -ves.

Chapter 65: Irregular Plurals, Part 1

There are no written exercises for this chapter.

Chapter 66: Irregular Plurals, Part 2

There are no written exercises for this chapter.

Chapter 67: Irregular Plurals, Part 3

I.

Students were instructed to write sentences with the plural of the following verbs. Answers will vary. The plural form of the words is given.

1.	man	men
2.	fisherman	fishermen
3.	deer	deer
4.	sheep	sheep
5.	child	children
6.	ox	oxen
7.	penny	pennies
8.	Miss Clark	The Misses Clarks *or* Miss Clarks
9.	Mr. Ray	Messrs. Ray
10.	Mrs. Ray	The Mrs. Rays
11.	cattle	cattle
12.	horseman	horsemen
13.	tooth	teeth
14.	German	Germans
15.	mouse	mice
16.	foot	feet
17.	brother (*both plurals*)	brothers, brethren
18.	Master Wilson	Masters Wilson
19.	Miss Atkins	The Misses Atkins *or* Miss Atkinses
20.	handful	handfuls
21.	son-in-law	sons-in-law
22.	man-of-war	men-of-war
23.	bluebird	bluebirds
24.	handkerchief	handkerchiefs

II.

Students were instructed to circle the plural nouns (bolded below), and write the singular on the blank line.

1. **Riches** do many **things.** <u>rich, thing</u>

2. **Tears** and **lamentations** were seen in almost every house. <u>tear, lamentation</u>
   (*Daniel Defoe (1660-1731), A Journal of the Plague Year*)

3. The skipper boasted of his catch of **fish.** <u>fish</u>

4. With **figs** and **plums** and Persian **dates** they fed me. <u>fig, plum, date</u>
   (*Thomas Hood (1799-1845), "The Plea of the Midsummer Fairies"*)

5. The rest of my **goods** were returned me. <u>good</u>
   (*Jonathan Swift (1667-1745), Gulliver's Travels*)

6. The **sheep** were browsing quietly on the low **hills.** <u>sheep, hill</u>

7. The **Messrs. Bertram** were very fine young **men.** <u>Mr. Bertram, man</u>
   (*Jane Austen (1775-1817), adapted from Mansfield Park*)

8. The admiration which the **Misses Thomas** felt for Mrs. Crawford was rapturous. <u>Miss Thomas</u>
   (*Jane Austen (1775-1817), adapted from Mansfield Park*)

9. He drew out the nail with a pair of **pincers**.   **(no singular form)**

10. His majesty marches northwards with a body of four thousand **horse**.   **horse**
    (*Daniel Defoe (1660-1731),* Memoirs of a Cavalier*)*

11. Flights of **doves** and **lapwings** were fluttering among the **leaves**.   **dove, lapwing, leaf**
    (*Thomas Moore (1779-1852),* The Epicurean*)*

12. Down fell the lady's thimble and **scissors** into the brook.   **(no singular form)**

13. The **Miss Blacks** lived, according to the worldly phrase, out of the world.   **Miss Black**
    (*Susan Ferrier (1782-1854),* The Inheritance*)*

14. The day after came the unfortunate **news** of the queen's death.   **(no singular form)**
    (*Jonathan Swift (1667-1745), "Letter to Lady Masham")*

15. No person dined with the queen but the two **princesses** royal.   **princess**
    (*Jonathan Swift (1667-1745),* Gulliver's Travels*)*

16. I cannot guess at the number of **ships**, but I think there must be several **hundreds** of sail.   **ship, hundred**
    (*Daniel Defoe (1660-1731),* A Journal of the Plague Year*)*

17. The **Miss Bertrams** continued to exercise their memories.   **Miss Bertram**
    (*Jane Austen (1775-1817),* Mansfield Park*)*

18. **Weavers, nailers, rope makers, artisans** of every degree and calling, thronged forward to join the procession from every gloomy and narrow street.   **weaver, nailer, rope maker, artisan**
    (*Sir Walter Scott (1771-1832),* Quentin Durward*)*

19. Now all the **youth** of England are on fire.   **youth**
    (*William Shakespeare (1564-1616),* Henry VI*)*

20. Charles has some talent for writing **verses**.   **verse**

Chapter 68: Personal Pronouns, Part 1

There are no written exercises for this chapter.

Chapter 69: Personal Pronouns, Part 2

I.

Students were instructed to underline personal pronouns and label person (1,2,3), gender (M, F, N or M/F), and number (S, P). *Note: The second person pronoun you is technically a plural form, even if used for a singular antecedent. However, we generally think of it as being singular when used for a singular antecedent. Students may identify this as singular, although if they mark it as the plural form, they are technically correct.*

1. **He (3, M, S)** was my friend, faithful and just to **me (1, M/F, S)**. *(William Shakespeare (1564-1616), Julius Caesar)*

2. Mahomet accompanied **his (3, M, S)** uncle on trading journeys. *(Thomas Carlyle (1795-1881), "The Hero as Prophet")*

3. **Our (1, M/F, P)** Clifford was a happy youth. *(William Wordsworth (1770-1850), "Song at the Feast of Brougham Castle...")*

4. And now, child, what art **thou (2, M/F, S)** doing?

5. **I (1, M/F, S)** think **I (1, M/F, S)** can guess what **you (2, M/F, P)** mean.

6. Then boast no more **your (2, M/F, P)** mighty deeds! *(James Shirley (1596-1666), "Death's Final Conquest")*

7. Round **him (3, M, S)** night resistless closes fast. *(James Thomson (1700-1748), "Winter")*

8. **I (1, M/F, S)** was in the utmost astonishment, and roared so loud that **they (3, M/F, P)** all ran back in fright. *(Jonathan Swift (1667-1745), Gulliver's Travels)*

9. **She (3, F, S)** listens, but **she (3, F, S)** cannot hear
    The foot of horse, the voice of man.
    (William Wordsworth (1770-1850), "The Idiot Boy")

10. **He (3, M, S)** hollowed a boat of the birchen bark,
    Which carried **him (3, M, S)** off from shore.
    (Thomas Moore (1779-1852), "The Lake of the Dismal Swamp")

11. At dead of night **their (3, M/F, P)** sails were filled. *(Arthur Hugh Clough (1819-1861), "Becalmed at Eve")*

12. Men at some time are masters of **their (3, M/F, P)** fates. *(William Shakespeare (1564-1616), Julius Caesar)*

13. Here is a sick man that would speak with **you (2, M/F, S)**. *(William Shakespeare (1564-1616), Julius Caesar)*

14. Why should **we (1, M/F, P)** yet **our (1, M/F, P)** sail unfurl? *(Thomas Moore (1779-1852), "Canadian Boat-Song")*

15. **I (1, M/F, S)** once more thought of attempting to break **my (1, M/F, S)** bonds. *(Jonathan Swift (1667-1745), Gulliver's Travels)*

16. **Our (1, M/F, P)** fortune and fame had departed. *(William Makepeace Thackeray (1811-1863), "The Chronicle of the Drum")*

17. The Hawbucks came in **their (3, M/F, P)** family coach, with the blood-red hand emblazoned all over **it (3, N, S)**. *(William Makepeace Thackeray (1811-1863), The Book of Snobs)*

18. The spoken word cannot be recalled. **It (3, N, S)** must go on **its (3, N, S)** way for good or evil. *(Thomas Hughes (1822-1896), Tom Brown at Oxford)*

19. **He (3, M, S)** saw the lake, and a meteor bright
    Quick over **its (3, N, S)** surface played.
    (Thomas Moore (1779-1852), "The Lake of the Dismal Swamp")

20. **I (1, M/F, S)** have endeavored to solve this difficulty another way.

21. The military part of **his (3, M, S)** life has furnished **him (3, M, S)** with many adventures. *(Joseph Addison (1672-1719), The Spectator)*

22. **He (3, M, S)** ambled alongside the footpath on which **they (3, M/F, P)** were walking, showing **his (3, M, S)** discomfort by a twist of **his (3, M, S)** neck every few seconds. *(Thomas Hughes (1822-1896), Tom Brown at Oxford)*

23. **Our (1, M/F, P)** provisions held out well, **our (1, M/F, P)** ship was stanch, and **our (1, M/F, P)** crew all in good health; but **we (1, M/F, P)** lay in the utmost distress for water. *(Jonathan Swift (1667-1745), Gulliver's Travels)*

24. Sweet day, so cool, so calm, so bright—
    The bridal of the earth and sky—
    The dew shall weep **thy (2, M/F, S)** fall tonight,
    For **thou (2, M/F, S)** must die.
    (George Herbert (1593-1632), "Virtue")

25. Lend **me (1, M/F, S)** **thy (2, M/F, S)** cloak, Sir Thomas. *(William Shakespeare (1564-1616), Henry V)*

26. Captain Fluellen, **you (2, M/F, S)** must come presently to the mines. The Duke of Gloucester would speak with **you**. **(2, M/F, S)** *(William Shakespeare (1564-1616), Henry V)*

27. Madam, what should **we (1, M/F, P)** do?

28. Worthy Macbeth, **we (1, M/F, P)** stay upon **your (2, M/F, S)** leisure. *(William Shakespeare (1564-1616), Macbeth)*

29. Fair and noble hostess,
    We (1, M/F, P) are **your (2, M/F, P)** guest tonight. *(William Shakespeare (1564-1616), Macbeth)*

II.
Students were instructed to label nominative case with N, genitive case with G, and objective case with O.

1. **He (N)** was my friend, faithful and just to **me (O)**. *(William Shakespeare (1564-1616), Julius Caesar)*

2. Mahomet accompanied **his (G)** uncle on trading journeys. *(Thomas Carlyle (1795-1881), "The Hero as Prophet")*

3. **Our (G)** Clifford was a happy youth. *(William Wordsworth (1770-1850), "Song at the Feast of Brougham Castle...")*

4. And now, child, what art **thou (N)** doing? *(Lord Byron (1788-1824), Letters and Journals of Lord Byron)*

5. **I (N)** think **I (N)** can guess what **you (N)** mean.

6. Then boast no more **your (G)** mighty deeds! *(James Shirley (1596-1666), "Death's Final Conquest")*

7. Round **him (O)** night resistless closes fast. *(James Thomson (1700-1748), "Winter")*

8. **I (N)** was in the utmost astonishment, and roared so loud that **they (N)** all ran back in fright. *(Jonathan Swift (1667-1745), Gulliver's Travels)*

9. **She (N)** listens, but **she (N)** cannot hear
   The foot of horse, the voice of man.
   (William Wordsworth (1770-1850), "The Idiot Boy")

10. **He (N)** hollowed a boat of the birchen bark,
    Which carried **him (O)** off from shore.
    (Thomas Moore (1779-1852), "The Lake of the Dismal Swamp")

11. At dead of night **their (G)** sails were filled. *(Arthur Hugh Clough (1819-1861), "Becalmed at Eve")*

12. Men at some time are masters of **their (G)** fates. *(William Shakespeare (1564-1616), Julius Caesar)*

13. Here is a sick man that would speak with **you (N)**. *(William Shakespeare (1564-1616), Julius Caesar)*

14. Why should **we (N)** yet **our (G)** sail unfurl? *(Thomas Moore (1779-1852), "Canadian Boat-Song")*

15. **I (N)** once more thought of attempting to break **my (G)** bonds. *(Jonathan Swift (1667-1745), Gulliver's Travels)*

16. **Our (G)** fortune and fame had departed. *(William Makepeace Thackeray (1811-1863), "The Chronicle of the Drum")*

17. The Hawbucks came in **their (G)** family coach, with the blood-red hand emblazoned all over **it (O)**. *(William Makepeace Thackeray (1811-1863), The Book of Snobs)*

18. The spoken word cannot be recalled. **It (N)** must go on **its (G)** way for good or evil. *(Thomas Hughes (1822-1896), Tom Brown at Oxford)*

19. **He (N)** saw the lake, and a meteor bright
    Quick over **its (G)** surface played.
    (Thomas Moore (1779-1852), "The Lake of the Dismal Swamp")

20. **I (N)** have endeavored to solve this difficulty another way.

21. The military part of **his (G)** life has furnished **him (O)** with many adventures. *(Joseph Addison (16672-1719), The Spectator)*

22. **He (N)** ambled alongside the footpath on which **they (N)** were walking, showing **his (G)** discomfort by a twist of **his (G)** neck every few seconds. *(Thomas Hughes (1822-1896), Tom Brown at Oxford)*

23. **Our (G)** provisions held out well, **our (G)** ship was stanch, and **our (G)** crew all in good health; but **we (N)** lay in the utmost distress for water. *(Jonathan Swift (1667-1745), Gulliver's Travels)*

24. Sweet day, so cool, so calm, so bright—
    The bridal of the earth and sky—
    The dew shall weep **thy (G)** fall tonight,
    For **thou (N)** must die.
    (George Herbert (1593-1632), "Virtue")

25. Lend **me (O)** **thy (G)** cloak, Sir Thomas. *(William Shakespeare (1564-1616), Henry V)*

26. Captain Fluellen, **you (N)** must come presently to the mines. The Duke of Gloucester would speak with **you. (O)** *(William Shakespeare (1564-1616), Henry V)*

27. Madam, what should **we (N)** do?

28. Worthy Macbeth, **we (N)** stay upon **your (G)** leisure. *(William Shakespeare (1564-1616), Macbeth)*

29. Fair and noble hostess,
    We (N) are **your (G)** guest tonight. *(William Shakespeare (1564-1616), Macbeth)*

III.
Students were instructed to underline each pronoun and label person, number, gender, and case.

1. A number of young people were assembled in the music room. **No pronouns** *(Maria Edgeworth (1768-1849), The Patronage)*

2. **He (3, S, M, N)** leads towards Rome a band of warlike Goths. *(William Shakespeare (1564-1616), Titus Andronicus)*

3. By ten o'clock the whole party were assembled at the Park. **No pronouns** *(Jane Austen (1775-1817), Sense and Sensibility)*

4. Have **I (1, S, M/F, N)** not reason to look pale and dead? *(William Shakespeare (1564-1616), King Richard II)*

5. People were terrified by the force of **their (3, P, M/F, G)** own imagination. *(Daniel Defoe (1660-1731), A Journal of the Plague Year)*

6. The Senate has letters from the general. **No pronouns** *(William Shakespeare (1564-1616), Coriolanus)*

7. **You (2, S, M/F, N)** misuse the reverence of your place. *(William Shakespeare (1564-1616), King Henry IV)*

8. There is hardly any place, or any company, where **you (2, S, M/F, N)** may not gain knowledge if **you (2, S, M/F, N)** please. *(Philip Dormer Stanhope, Earl of Chesterfield (1694-1773), "Lord Chesterfield's Letters")*

9. Here comes another troop to seek for **you (2, S, M/F, O)**. *(William Shakespeare (1564-1616), Othello)*

10. **Their (3, P, M/F, G)** mastiffs are of unmatchable courage. *(William Shakespeare (1564-1616), Henry V)*

11. **Our (1, P, M/F, G)** family dined in the field, and **we (1, P, M/F, N)** sat, or rather reclined, round a temperate repast. *(Oliver Goldsmith (1730-1774), The Vicar of Wakefield)*

12. **Our (1, P, M/F, G)** society will not break up, but **we (1, P, M/F, N)** shall settle in some other place. *(William Cowper (1731-1800), "Letters")*

13. Let nobody blame **him (3, S, M, O)**; **his (3, S, M, G)** scorn **I (1, S, M/F, N)** approve. *(William Shakespeare (1564-1616), Othello)*

14. The Senate have concluded
    To give this day a crown to mighty Caesar. **No pronouns**
    (William Shakespeare (1564-1616), Julius Caesar)

15. **He (3, S, M, N)** is banished, as enemy to the people and **his (3, S, M, G)** country. *(William Shakespeare (1564-1616), Coriolanus)*

16. Society has been called the happiness of life. **No pronouns**

17. **His (3, S, M, G)** army is a ragged multitude
    Of hinds and peasants, rude and merciless.
    (William Shakespeare (1564-1616), King Henry IV)

18. There is a great difference between knowledge and wisdom. **No pronouns**

19. All the country in a general voice cried hate upon **him (3, S, M, O)**. *(William Shakespeare (1564-1616), King Henry IV)*

20. The king hath called **his (3, S, M, G)** Parliament. *(William Shakespeare (1564-1616), King Henry IV)*

21. Let all the number of the stars give light to **thy (2, S, M/F, G)** fair way! *(William Shakespeare (1564-1616), Antony and Cleopatra)*

IV.
Check the student's sentences to be sure they used the pronouns correctly. Answers will vary.

Chapter 70: Nominative and Objective Case

Students were instructed to underline the substantives that are subjects and label them N for nominative case. They are underlined below. They were to circle the substantives that are objects and label them O for objective case. They are bolded below.

1. Forth on his fiery **steed** betimes <u>he</u> rode. (*John Dryden (1631-1700), "Palamon and Arcite," a poem retelling the "A Knight's Tale"*)

2. A thick <u>forest</u> lay near the **city**. (*John Dryden (1631-1700), "Palamon and Arcite"*)

3. When <u>they</u> met, <u>they</u> made a surly **stand**. (*John Dryden (1631-1700), "Palamon and Arcite"*)

4. <u>It</u> is true, <u>hundreds</u>, yea <u>thousands</u> of **families** fled away at this last **plague**. (*Daniel Defoe (1660-1731), A Journal of the Plague Year*)

5. <u>Some</u> of these **rambles** led **me** to great **distances**. (*Thomas De Quincey (1785-1859), Confessions of an English Opium-Eater*)

6. When the moonlight <u>nights</u> returned, <u>we</u> used to venture into the **desert**. (*Thomas Moore (1779-1852), The Epicurean*)

7. <u>He</u> loaded a great **wagon** with **hay**. (*Sir Walter Scott (1771-1832), Tales of a Grandfather*)

8. With her two **brothers** this fair <u>lady</u> dwelt. (*John Keats (1795-1821), "Isabella"*)

9. The <u>lord</u> of the **castle** in **wrath** arose.

10. The fair <u>breeze</u> blew, the white <u>foam</u> flew,
    The <u>furrow</u> followed free;
    <u>We</u> were the first <u>that</u> ever burst
    Into that silent **sea**.
    (*Samuel Taylor Coleridge (1722-1834), "The Rime of the Ancient Mariner"*)

11. A dense <u>fog</u> shrouded the **landscape**.

12. How <u>he</u> blessed this little Polish **lady**! (*William Black (1841-1898), Sunset*)

Chapter 71: Predicate Nominative

There were no written exercises for chapter 71. Students were asked to review chapters 43-46.

Chapter 72: Nominative in Exclamations

I.
Students were instructed to repeat the exercises from chapter 15.

1. O learned sir, (**V**)
   <u>You and your learning</u> I <u>revere</u>.
   (William Cowper (1731-1800), "The Ninth Satire of the First Book of Horace")

2. <u>The good old man</u>
   <u>Means no offense</u>, sweet lady (**V**)!
   (Samuel Taylor Coleridge (1722-1834), Zapolya)

3. Goodbye! <u>(You)</u> <u>Drive on</u>, coachman (**V**).

4. <u>Why</u>, Sir John (**V**), <u>my face</u> <u>does you no harm</u>.

5. Good cousin (**V**), <u>(You)</u> <u>give me audience for a while</u>.

6. <u>Yours is</u> the prize, victorious prince (**V**).

7. "<u>(You)</u> <u>Wake</u>, Allan-bane (**V**)," aloud <u>she</u> <u>cried</u>
   <u>To the old minstrel by her side</u>.
   (Sir Walter Scott (1771-1832), "Lady of the Lake")

8. <u>(You)</u> <u>Bid adieu</u>, my sad heart (**V**), <u>bid adieu to thy peace</u>. *(William Cowper (1731-1800), "On Delia")*

9. My dear little cousin (**V**), <u>what can be</u> the matter?

10. <u>(You)</u> <u>Come</u>, Evening (**V**), <u>once again</u>, season of peace (**V**)! *(William Cowper (1731-1800), "Evening")*

11. <u>Plain truth</u>, dear Murray (**V**), <u>needs no flowers of speech</u>. *(Alexander Pope, The Sixth Epistle of the First Book of Horace, "To Mr. Murray")*

12. <u>(You)</u> <u>Permit me now</u>, Sir William (**V**), <u>to address myself personally to you</u>. *(Letter III to Sir William Draper from Junius, 1769)*

13. <u>(You)</u> <u>Go</u>, my dread lord (**V**), <u>to your great-grandsire's tomb</u>. *(Shakespeare (1564-1616), Henry V)*

14. <u>Why do</u> <u>you</u> <u>stay so long</u>, my lords of France (**V**)? *(William Shakespeare, (1564-1616) Henry V)*

15. My pretty cousins (**V**), <u>you</u> <u>mistake me much</u>. *(Shakespeare (1564-1616), Richard III)*

16. <u>(You)</u> <u>Come on</u>, Lord Hastings (**V**). <u>Will</u> <u>you</u> <u>go with me</u>? *(Shakespeare (1564-1616), Richard III)*

17. O Romeo (**V**), Romeo (**V**), <u>brave Mercutio's</u> <u>dead</u>. *(Shakespeare (1564-1616), Romeo and Juliet)*
    Note: The contraction Mercutio's makes it easy to miss the verb is. Compare, "<u>Mercutio</u> <u>is dead</u>."

18. <u>I</u> <u>will avenge this insult</u>, noble queen (**V**). *(Alfred, Lord Tennyson (1809-1892), Idylls of the King)*

19. O friend (**V**), <u>I</u> <u>seek a harborage for the night</u>. *(Alfred, Lord Tennyson (1809-1892), Idylls of the King)*

20. My lord (**V**), <u>I</u> <u>saw three bandits by the rock</u>. *(Alfred, Lord Tennyson (1809-1892), Idylls of the King)*

21. Father! (**V**) <u>thy days</u> <u>have passed in peace</u>. *(Lord Byron (1788-1824), "The Giaour")*

II.
Students were instructed to underline all the vocatives and circle all the exclamatory nominatives (bolded below).

1. Roll on, <u>thou deep and dark-blue ocean</u>, **roll**! *(Lord Byron (1788-1824), "The Ocean")*
2. **Weapons! Arms!** What's the matter here? *(William Shakespeare (1564-1616), King Lear)*
3. <u>Tartar, and Saphi, and Turcoman,</u>
   Strike your tents and throng to the van.
   (Lord Byron (1788-1824), "The Siege of Corinth")
4. Awake! **what ho**, <u>Brabantio</u>! **thieves! thieves! thieves!** *(William Shakespeare (1564-1616), Othello)*
5. She, <u>poor wretch</u>! for grief can speak no more. *(William Shakespeare (1564-1616), King Henry VI)*
6. <u>Fair daffodils</u>, we weep to see
   You haste away so soon.
   (Robert Herrick (1591-1674), "To Daffodils")
7. Weep no more, <u>woeful shepherds</u>, weep no more. *(John Milton (1608-1674), "Lycidas")*
8. <u>O father</u>! I am young and very happy.
9. **O wonder!** how many goodly creatures are there here! *(William Shakespeare (1564-1616), The Tempest)*
10. <u>Milton</u>! thou should'st be living at this hour. *(William Wordsworth (1770-1850), "Sonnet to Milton")*
11. **Liberty! freedom!** Tyranny is dead! *(William Shakespeare (1564-1616), Julius Caesar)*
12. Farewell, <u>ye dungeons dark and strong</u>. *(Robert Burns (1759-1796), "McPherson's Farewell")*

III.
Be sure to check that the nouns were used as vocatives and exclamatory nominatives properly. Answers will vary.

IV.
Students were instructed to analyze the sentences in II.

1. <u>(You) (S)</u> <u>Roll **(Pred)** on **(Adv)**</u>, (thou deep and dark-blue ocean)**(V)**, <u>roll **(Pred)**</u>! *(Lord Byron (1788-1824), "The Ocean")*
2. (Weapons! Arms!) **(E)** <u>What's (what-**S**, is-**Pred**) the **(Adj)** matter **(PN)** here **(Adv)**</u>? *(William Shakespeare (1564-1616), King Lear)*
3. (Tartar, and Saphi, and Turcoman) **(V)**,
   <u>(you) **(S)** strike **(Pred)** your **(Adj)** tents **(DO)** and **(C)** throng **(Pred)** (to the van) **(Adv)**</u>.
   (Lord Byron (1788-1824), "The Siege of Corinth")
4. <u>(You) **(S)** Awake! **(Pred)**</u> (what ho) **(E)**, (Brabantio!) **(V)** (thieves! thieves! thieves!) **(E)** *(William Shakespeare (1564-1616), Othello)*
5. <u>She **(S)**</u>, (poor wretch!) **(V)** <u>(for grief) **(Adv)** (can speak) **(Pred)** no **(Adv)** more **(Adv)**</u>. *(William Shakespeare (1564-1616), King Henry VI)*
6. (Fair daffodils)**(V)**, <u>we **(S)** weep **(Pred)** (to see) **(Adv)**</u>*
   <u>You **(S)** haste **(Pred)** away **(Adv)** so **(Adv)** soon **(Adv)**</u>.
   (Robert Herrick (1591-1674), "To Daffodils")
7. <u>(You) **(S)** Weep **(Pred)** no **(Adv)** more **(Adv)**</u>, (woeful shepherds)**(V)**, <u>weep **(Pred)** no **(Adv)** more **(Adv)**</u>. *(John Milton (1608-1674), "Lycidas")*
8. (O father!) **(V)** <u>I **(S)** am **(Pred)** young **(PA)** and **(C)** very **(Adv)** happy **(PA)**</u>.

9. (O wonder!) (**E**) <u>how (**Adv**) many (**Adj**) goodly (**Adj**) creatures (**S**) are (**Pred**) there (**Adv**) here (**Adv**)</u>! *(William Shakespeare (1564-1616), The Tempest)*

10. (Milton!) (**V**) <u>thou (**S**) (should'st be living) (**Pred**) (at this hour) (**Adv**)</u>. *(William Wordsworth (1770-1850), "Sonnet to Milton")*

11. (Liberty! freedom!) (**E**) <u>Tyranny (**S**) is (**Pred**) dead (**PA**)</u>! *(William Shakespeare (1564-1616), Julius Caesar)*

12. <u>(You) (**S**) Fare (**Pred**) well (**Adv**)</u>, (ye dungeons dark and strong) (**V**). *(Robert Burns (1759-1796), "McPherson's Farewell")*

*Infinitives are studied in chapter 100. Students may not be able to identify this infinitive, but help them see it is not the verb.

Chapter 72: Additional Review Exercises

Students were instructed to underline the nominatives (all nouns or pronouns in nominative case) in the following sentences and parse them.

1. The <u>moonbeams</u> streamed on the tall tower of St. Mark.
   <u>moonbeams: Sub, N, P</u>
   (Washington Irving (1783-1859), Tales of a Traveler)

2. Their <u>parents</u> were respectable <u>farmers</u>.
   <u>parents: Sub, M/F, P</u>　　　**<u>farmers: PN, M/F, P</u>**

3. A cold <u>chill</u> ran through Sam's veins.
   <u>chill: Sub, N, S</u>
   (Washington Irving (1783-1859), Tales of a Traveler)

4. The <u>crowd</u> was dispersed, and <u>several</u> of the rioters were slain.
   <u>crowd: Sub, N, S</u>　　　**<u>several: Sub, N, P</u>**
   (Lord Thomas Macaulay (1800-1859), History of England)

5. Howling <u>Winter</u> fled afar.
   <u>Winter: Sub, N, S</u>
   (Thomas Campbell (1777-1844), "Ode to Winter")

6. Poor <u>Cinderella</u>! Her <u>life</u> was very hard.
   <u>Cinderella: V, F, S</u>　　　**<u>life: Sub, N, S</u>**

7. <u>Captain Brown</u> and his two <u>daughters</u> lived in a small house on the outskirts of the village.
   <u>Captain Brown: Sub, M, S</u>　　　**<u>daughters: Sub, F, P</u>**
   (Elizabeth Gaskell (1810-1865), Cranford)

8. O ye wild <u>groves</u>, O, where is now your <u>bloom</u>?
   <u>groves: V, N, P</u>　　　**<u>bloom: Sub, N, S</u>**
   (James Beattie (1735-1803), "Life and Immortality")

9. Auspicious <u>Hope</u>, in thy sweet garden grow
   <u>Hope: V, F, S</u>
   Wreaths for each toil, a charm for every woe.
   (Thomas Campbell (1777-1844), "Pleasures of Hope")

10. The <u>haymakers</u> were at work in the fields, and the <u>perfume</u> of the new-mown hay brought with it the recollection of my home.
    <u>haymakers: Sub, M/F, P</u>　　　**<u>perfume: Sub, N, S</u>**
    (Washington Irving (1783-1859), Tales of a Traveler)

11. My <u>uncle</u> listened with inward impatience while the little <u>marquis</u> descanted, with his usual fire and vivacity, on the achievements of his ancestors, whose <u>portraits</u> hung along the wall.
    <u>uncle: Sub, M, S</u>　　　**<u>marquis: Sub, M, S</u>**　　　**<u>portraits: Sub, N, P</u>**
    (Washington Irving (1783-1859), Tales of a Traveler)

12. Every <u>visitor</u> who arrived after nightfall was challenged from a loophole or from a barricaded window.
    <u>visitor: Sub, M/F, S</u>
    (Lord Thomas Macaulay (1800-1859), History of England)

13. The <u>Romans</u> were, in their origin, <u>banditti</u>.
    <u>Romans: Sub, M/F, P</u>　　　**<u>banditti: PN, M, P</u>**

14. Her <u>father</u> dwelt where yonder <u>castle</u> shines
    father: Sub, M, S   castle: Sub, N, S
    O'er clust'ring trees and terrace-mantling vines.
    (Thomas Campbell (1777-1844), "Theodric")

15. Delay not, <u>Caesar</u>. Read it instantly.
    Caesar: V, M, S
    (William Shakespeare (1564-1616), Julius Caesar*)*

Chapter 73: Genitive or Possessive Case

I.

Students were instructed to make the following words into genitives with a noun attached. The genitive for each noun is given. Nouns attached, such as "Jones's **house**," will vary.

1. Jones   Jones's (see Section 306 for the one-syllable rule)
2. Thomas   Thomas' (*or* Thomas's, see Section 306 in text)
3. Gibbs   Gibbs's
4. Cyrus   Cyrus (*or* Cyrus's)
5. Charles   Charles's
6. Caesar   Caesar's
7. Julius   Julius' (*or* Julius's)
8. Mr. Converse   Mr. Converse's
9. Mr. Conners   Mr. Conners' (*or* Mr. Conners's)
10. Mrs. Ross   Mrs. Ross's
11. Charles Foss   Charles Foss's
12. Antonius   Antonius' (*or* Antonius's)
13. Brutus   Brutus (*or* Brutus's)
14. Cassius   Cassius (*or* Cassius's)
15. Mr. Anthony Brooks   Mr. Anthony Brooks's
16. J. T. Fields   J. T. Fields's
17. Romulus   Romulus' (*or* Romulus's)
18. Remus   Remus' (*or* Remus's)
19. Mr. Strangways   Mr. Strangways' (*or* Strangways's)
20. Mrs. Smithers   Mrs. Smithers' (*or* Mrs. Smithers's)
21. Matthew   Matthew's
22. John Matthews   John Matthews' (*or* Matthews's)
23. Dr. Morris   Dr. Morris' (*or* Morris's)
24. Maurice   Maurice's
25. Lord Douglas   Lord Douglas' (*or* Douglas's)
26. Dr. Ellis   Dr. Ellis' (*or* Ellis's)
27. James   James's
28. Francis   Francis' (*or* Francis's)
29. Frances   Frances' (*or* Frances's)
30. Eunice   Eunice's
31. Felix   Felix' (*or* Felix's)
32. Rose   Rose's

II.

Check for proper genitives. Answers will vary.

III.

Review chapter 35, Exercise II.

IV.

The singular and plural genitive form is shown. Students should attach a noun.

1. horse   horse's bridle   horses' bridle
2. man   man's   men's

3.	woman	woman's	women's
4.	child	child's	children's
5.	fish	fish's	fish's
6.	gentleman	gentleman's	gentlemen's
7.	deer	deer's	deer's
8.	sheep	sheep's	sheep's
9.	bird	bird's	birds'
10.	wolf	wolf's	wolves'
11.	calf	calf's	calves'
12.	tiger	tiger's	tigers'
13.	snake	snake's	snakes'
14.	badger	badger's	badgers'
15.	fly	fly's	flies'
16.	spy	spy's	spies'
17.	turkey	turkey's	turkeys'
18.	donkey	donkey's	donkeys'
19.	ally	ally's	allies'

V.

Students were instructed to underline all the genitives and all the *of*-phrases and draw an arrow to what noun or pronoun each belongs (bolded below).

Chapter 33, I

1. The emperor's **palace** is in the **center** of the city, where the two great streets meet. *(Jonathan Swift (1667-1745), Gulliver's Travels)*

2. Oliver's **education** began when he was about three years old.*(Washington Irving (1783-1859), Oliver Goldsmith)*

3. Caesar scorns the poet's **lays**. *(Alexander Pope (1688-1744), "Satire")*

4. The silver light, with quivering glance.
   Played on the water's still **expanse**.
   (Sir Walter Scott (1771-1832), "Lady of the Lake")

5. Here on this beach a hundred years ago,
   Three **children** of three houses, Annie Lee,
   The prettiest little damsel in the port,
   And Philip Ray, the miller's only **son**,
   And Enoch Arden, a rough sailor's **lad**,
   Made orphan by a winter shipwreck, played
   Among the **waste** and **lumber** of the shore.
   (Alfred, Lord Tennyson (1809-1892), "Enoch Arden")

6. It is not the **greatness** of a man's **means** that makes him independent, so much as the **smallness** of his wants.
   (William Cobbett (1763-1835))

7. In faith and hope the world will disagree.
   But all mankind's **concern** is charity.
   (Alexander Pope (1688-1744), "Essay on Man")

8. The jester's **speech** made the duke laugh. *(Sir Walter Scott (1771-1832), Quentin Durward)*

9. A man's **nature** runs either to herbs or weeds. *(Francis Bacon (1561-1626), "Essays, Civil and Moral")*

Chapter 33, IV

1. The <u>monarch's</u> **wrath** began to rise. *(Lord Byron (1788-1824), "Siege and Conquest of Alhama")*

2. They err who imagine that this <u>man's</u> **courage** was ferocity. *(Thomas Carlyle (1795-1881),* Spiritual Portrait of Luther*)*

3. Two <u>years'</u> **travel** in distant and barbarous countries has accustomed me to bear privations.*(Lord Byron (1788-1824), "Byron's Reflections on Himself")*

4. Hark! hark! the lark at <u>heaven's</u> **gate** sings. *(William Shakespeare (1564-1616),* Cymbeline*)*

5. Portia dressed herself and her maid in <u>men's</u> **apparel**. *(Charles and Mary Lamb's* Tales from Shakespeare, *"Merchant of Venice")*

6. He waved his <u>huntsman's</u> **cap** on high. *(Sir Walter Scott (1771-1832), "The Wild Hunter")*

7. The <u>Porters'</u> **visit** was all but over. *(Thomas Hughes (1822-1896),* Tom Brown at Oxford*)*

8. The <u>ladies'</u> **colds** kept them at home all the evening.

9. The crags repeat the <u>ravens'</u> **croak**. *(William Wordsworth (1770-1850), "Fidelity")*

10. <u>Farmer Grove's</u> **house** is on fire!

11. The Major paced the terrace in **front** <u>of the house</u> for his two <u>hours'</u> constitutional **walk**. *(William Makepeace Thackeray (1811-1863),* History of Pendennis)

VI.
Oral exercise. As your student does this exercise orally, review Section 307 together and decide if the change to the *of*-phrase, or to the *'s*, is better or worse, or equally acceptable.

Chapter 74: Case of Appositives

I.

Students were instructed to review the exercises from chapter 37, reproduced below. They should fill in the blanks again with nouns for their appositives (suggestions are given below). They were to underline the appositives and label the case of each appositive, N for nominative case, O for objective case.

<u>Chapter 37, I</u>

1. Mr. Jones, **the contractor**, is building a house for me. (**N**)
2. Have you seen Rover, **my dog**, anywhere? (**O**)
3. Animals of all kinds, **monkeys, lions, tigers, and hippos**, were exhibited in the menagerie. (**N**)
4. Chapman, **the captain of the team**, broke his collar bone. (**N**)
5. My new kite, **a gift from my uncle**, is caught in the tree. (**N**)
6. Washington, **the President of the United States**, is on the Potomac. (**N**)
7. Who has met my young friend **Jack** today? (**O**)
8. Charles I, **King of England**, was beheaded in 1649. (**N**)
9. Washington, **the President of his country**, was born in 1732. (**N**)
10. Tiger-hunting, **a dangerous pursuit**, was the sultan's chief delight. (**N**)

<u>Chapter 37, II</u>

1. An Englishwoman, **the wife of one of the officers (N)**, was sitting on the battlements with her child in her arms. *(Sir Walter Scott (1771-1832), History of Scotland)*
2. I went to visit Mr. Hobbes, **the famous philosopher (O)**. *(Samuel Pepys (1633-1703), Diary)*
3. We were hopeful boys, **all three of us (N)**. *(Daniel Defoe (1660-1731), The Life of Colonel Jack)*
4. Spring, **the sweet Spring (N)**, is the year's pleasant king. *(Thomas Nash (1567-1601), "Spring")*
5. Then forth they all out of their baskets drew
    Great store of flowers, **the honor of the field (O)**.
    (Edmund Spenser (1552-1599), "Prothalamion")
6. He was speedily summoned to the apartment of his captain, **the Lord Crawford (O).** *(Sir Walter Scott (1771-1832), Quentin Durward)*
7. No rude sound shall reach thine ear,
    Armor's clang and war-steed champing (N).
    (Sir Walter Scott (1771-1832), "Song")
    Note: The appositive modifies sound.
8. And thus spake on that ancient man,
    The bright-eyed mariner (N).
    (Samuel Taylor Coleridge (1722-1834), "The Rime of the Ancient Mariner")
9. There lived at no great distance from this stronghold a farmer, **a bold and stout man (N)**, whose name was Binnock. *(Sir Walter Scott (1771-1832), History of Scotland)*

II.
Students were instructed to underline the appositives and label the case of each (nominative with N, objective with O)

1. I visited my old friend and fellow-traveler, **Mr. Henshaw (O).** *(John Evelyn (1620-1706), "The Diary of John Evelyn")*

2. At length the day dawned, **— that dreadful day (N)**. *(Thomas Moore (1779-1852), The Epicurean)*

3. 'Twas where the madcap duke **his uncle (N)** kept. *(William Shakespeare (1564-1616), King Henry IV)*

4. So off they scampered, **man and horse (N)**. *(Thomas Hood (1799-1845), "The Epping Hunt")*

5. The north wind, **that welcome visitor (N),** freshened the air. *(Thomas Moore (1779-1852), The Epicurean)*

6. I see him yet, **the princely boy (O)**!

7. His prayer he saith, **this patient, holy man (N)**. *(John Keats (1795-1821), "The Eve of St. Agnes")*

8. The vices of authority are chiefly four: **delays, corruption, roughness, and facility (N)**. *(Francis Bacon (1561-1626), "Essays, Civil and Moral")*

9. 'T is past, **that melancholy dream (N)**! *(William Wordsworth (1770-1850), "I Traveled Among Unknown Men")*

10. Campley, **a friend of mine (N),** came by. *(William Cowper (1731-1800), "The Ninth Satire of the First Book of Horace")*

11. The mayor, **an aged man (N),** made an address.

12. He lent me his only weapon, **a sword (O).**

13. Captain William Robinson, **a Cornishman (N), [commander of the "Hopewell," (a stout ship of three hundred tons)(O),](N)** came to my house. *Note: "a stout ship of three hundred tons" is an appositive modifying "Hopewell" and therefore it is in the objective case, but it is nested inside the appositive modifying "Captain William Robinson."*
    (Jonathan Swift (1667-1745), Gulliver's Travels)

III.
Students were instructed to analyze each of the sentences from Exercise II, which are reproduced below.

1. I **(S)** visited **(Pred)** my **(Adj)** old **(Adj)** friend **(compound DO)** and **(C)** fellow-traveler **(compound DO),** Mr. Henshaw **(App-Adj)**. *(John Evelyn (1620-1706), "The Diary of John Evelyn")*

2. (At length) **(Adv)** the **(Adj)** day **(S)** dawned **(Pred),** — (that dreadful day) **(App-Adj)**. *(Thomas Moore (1779-1852), The Epicurean)*

3. 'T **(S)** was **(Pred)** [where **(Adv)** the **(Adj)** madcap **(Adj)** duke **(S)** (his **(Adj)** uncle)**(App-Adj)** kept **(V)**]. *(William Shakespeare (1564-1616), King Henry IV)*

4. So **(Adv)** off **(Adv)** they **(S)** scampered **(Pred),** (man and horse) **(App-Adj)**. *(Thomas Hood (1799-1845), "The Epping Hunt")*

5. The **(Adj)** north **(Adj)** wind **(S),** (that welcome visitor) **(App-Adj),** freshened **(Pred)** the **(Adj)** air **(DO)**. *(Thomas Moore (1779-1852), The Epicurean)*

6. I **(S)** see **(Pred)** him **(DO)** yet **(Adv),** (the princely boy) **(App-Adj)**!

7. His **(Adj)** prayer **(DO)** he **(S)** saith **(Pred),** (this patient, holy man) **(App-Adj)**. *(John Keats (1795-1821), "The Eve of St. Agnes")*

8. The (**Adj**) vices (**S**) (of authority) (**Adj**) are (**Pred**) chiefly (**Adv**) four (**PN**): delays, corruption, roughness, and facility (**App-Adj**). *(Francis Bacon (1561-1626), "Essays, Civil and Moral")*

9. 'T (**S**) is (**Pred**) past (**PA**), (that melancholy dream) (**App-Adj**)! *(William Wordsworth (1770-1850), "I Traveled Among Unknown Men")*

10. Campley (**S**), (a friend of mine) (**App-Adj**), came (**Pred**) by (**Adv**). *(William Cowper (1731-1800), "The Ninth Satire of the First Book of Horace")*

11. The (**Adj**) mayor (**S**), (an aged man) (**App-Adj**), made (**Pred**) an (**Adj**) address (**DO**).

12. He (**S**) lent (**Pred**) me (**IO**) his (**Adj**) only (**Adj**) weapon (**DO**), (a sword) (**App-Adj**).

13. (Captain William Robinson)(**S**), (a Cornishman) (**App-Adj**), [commander (of the "Hopewell,") (a stout ship of three hundred tons)(**App-Adj**),](**App-Adj**) came (**Pred**) (to my house)(**Adv**). *(Jonathan Swift (1667-1745), Gulliver's Travels)*

Chapter 75: Indirect Object

I.

Students were instructed to fill in the blanks with indirect objects. Answers will vary. Suggestions are given.

1. My sister gave __me__ a book.
2. A deserter brought __me__ news of the battle.
3. The king granted __him__ a pension of a hundred pounds.
4. Alfred will show __John__ his collection of postage stamps.
5. The governor paid __the citizen__ the reward.
6. The prisoner told __me__ the whole story.
7. De Quincey's father left __him__ a large sum of money.
8. Our teacher granted __us__ our request.
9. Can such conduct give __you__ any satisfaction?
10. His indulgent father forgave __him__ his many faults.
11. The grocer refused __him__ credit.
12. The surly porter refused __him__ permission to enter the building.

II.

Students were instructed to circle all the direct objects that they find (bolded here), and underline the phrases in which the idea of the indirect object is expressed by means of *to*. They were to draw an arrow from the direct object to the indirect object.

1. He by will bequeathed his **lands** to me. (*William Shakespeare (1564-1616),* King Henry IV)
2. To Mortimer will I declare these **tidings**.
3. He has told all his **troubles** to you.
4. Entrust your **message** to her.
5. Do you give **attention** to my words?
6. The judges awarded the **prize** to Oliver.
7. Do you ascribe this **drama** to Shakespeare?
8. Show the **drawing** to your teacher.
9. The scout made his **report** to the officer.

III.

Students were instructed to make ten sentences containing the following verbs, with both a direct and an indirect object. Check to be sure the verbs are used with indirect and direct objects. Answers will vary.

IV.

Students were instructed to underline the subject once and the predicate twice, circle the direct objects (shown in bold print), and draw an arrow from the direct object to the indirect objects (shown in parentheses).

1. I shall assign (you) the **post** of danger and of renown. (*William Godwin (1756-1836), "St. Leon"*)
2. The king ordered (him) a small **present** and dismissed **him**.
3. The thoughts of the day gave my (mind) **employment** for the whole night.

4. <u>Miss Pratt</u>   <u>gave (Uncle Adam) a **jog** on the elbow</u>. *(Susan Ferrier (1782-1854),* The Inheritance*)*

5. <u>The king</u>   <u>made (me) a **present**</u>.

6. <u>I</u>   <u>will bring (you) certain **news** from Shrewsbury</u>. *(William Shakespeare (1564-1616),* King Henry IV*)*

7. <u>I</u>   <u>will deny (thee) **nothing**</u>. *(William Shakespeare (1564-1616),* King Henry IV*)*

8. <u>(You)</u>   <u>Fetch (me) the **hat** and **rapier** in my cell</u>. *(William Shakespeare (1564-1616),* The Tempest*)*

9. <u>(You)</u>   <u>Forgive (us) our **sins**</u>! *(Derived from Matthew 6:12)*

10. <u>My father</u>   <u>gave (him) **welcome**</u>. *(William Shakespeare (1564-1616),* King Henry IV*)*

11. <u>I</u>   <u>will not lend (thee) a **penny**</u>. *(William Shakespeare (1564-1616),* Merry Wives of Windsor*)*

12. <u>The mayor</u>   <u>in courtesy showed (me) the **castle**</u>. *(William Shakespeare (1564-1616),* Richard III*)*

13. <u>I</u>   <u>shall tell (you) a pretty **tale**</u>. *(William Shakespeare (1564-1616),* Coriolanus*)*

14. <u>(You)</u>   <u>Vouchsafe (me) one fair **look**</u>. *(William Shakespeare (1564-1616),* Two Gentlemen of Verona*)*

15. <u>The reading</u>   <u>of those volumes afforded (me) much **amusement**</u>. *(William Cowper (1731-1800), "Cowper's Letters")*

16. <u>I</u>   <u>have occasioned (her) some **confusion**, and, for the moment, a little **resentment**</u>. *(Fanny Burney (1752-1840),* Cecilia: Or Memoirs of an Heiress*)*

17. <u>He</u>   <u>'ll make (her) two or three fine **speeches**</u>, and then <u>she</u>   <u>'ll be perfectly contented</u>. *(Fanny Burney (1752-1840),* Cecilia: Or Memoirs of an Heiress*)*

18. <u>Voltaire, who was then in England,</u>   <u>sent (him) a **letter** of consolation</u>. *(Samuel Johnson (1709-1784), "The Lives of English Poets")*

19. <u>The evening</u>   <u>had afforded (Edmund) little **pleasure**</u>. *(Jane Austen (1775-1817),* Mansfield Park*)*

20. <u>Mrs. St. Clair</u>   <u>here wished the happy (pair) **good morning**</u>. *(Susan Ferrier (1782-1854),* The Inheritance*)*

A. Punctuation Practice Exercises

The proper capitalization and punctuation is shown.

1. "It will be midnight," said the coachman, "before we arrive at our inn."

2. We give thee heart and hand,
   Our glorious native land.
   (Bayard Taylor (1825-1878), "The Song of 1876")

3. Yet though destruction sweep those lovely plains,
   Rise fellow-men, our country yet remains!
   (Thomas Campbell (1777-1844), "The Pleasures of Hope")

4. After a dreadful night of anxiety, perplexity, and peril, the darkness slowly disappeared. *(Edward John Trelawny (1792-1881),* Adventures of a Younger Son)

5. As he that lives longest lives but a little while, every man may be certain that he has no time to waste. *(Samuel Johnson (1709-1784), "Selected Writings")*

6. At its western side is a deep ravine or valley, through which a small stream rushes. *(George Henry Borrow (1803-1881),* The Bible in Spain)

B. Punctuation Practice Exercises

The proper capitalization and punctuation is shown.

1. "The Vision of Sir Launfal" was written by James Russell Lowell.

2. "Will not your trip to Bath afford you an opportunity to visit us at Weston?"

3. "That is my brother," said Jack.

4. Dr. Adams, the eminent surgeon, took charge of the case.

5. We ran on, the dogs pursuing us, until we reached the bridge.

6. A quotation, especially if it is a long quotation, should always be to the point.

7. She hastened downstairs, ordered the servants to arm themselves with the weapons first at hand, placed herself at their head, and returned immediately. *(Washington Irving (1783-1859),* The Adventure of My Aunt)

C. Punctuation Practice Exercises

Here is the selection properly capitalized and punctuated.

The boys were glad to find a blazing fire awaiting them upon their return to the Red Lion. Carl and his party were there first. Soon afterward Peter and Jacob came in. They had inquired in vain concerning Dr. Boekman. All they could ascertain was that he had been seen in Haarlem that morning.
--MARY MAPES, HANS BRINKER OR THE SILVER SKATES

D. Punctuation Practice Exercises

Here is the selection properly capitalized and punctuated.

On January 2, we had made 11,340 miles, or 5,250 French leagues, since our starting-point in the Japan seas. Before the ship's head stretched the dangerous shores of the coral sea, on the northeast coast of Australia. Our boat lay along some miles from the redoubtable bank on which Cook's vessel was lost, June 10, 1770. The boat in which Cook was struck on a rock, and if it did not sink, it was owing to a piece of the coral that was broken by the shock, and fixed itself in the broken keel.
-JULES VERNE, TWENTY THOUSAND LEAGUES UNDER THE SEA

Made in the USA
Middletown, DE
07 November 2018